How to Start Up and Manage Your Own Hair Salon

... and Make it BIG in the Salon Business

• • • • • • • • • • • • • •

**Tips, Tricks and Secrets
to Get More Clients into Your Chair!**

By Linda L. Chappo

Cover Design: Linda Chappo
Publisher: Heart to Heart Living
ISBN: 978-0-9823279-5-1
Copyright ©2011

For more information, contact:
Linda L. Chappo
lchappo@aol.com

Other Books by Linda L. Chappo

Full Strength Marketing:
How You Can Use Your Hidden Strengths,
Break Through Barriers,
and Raise Your Profits
(Co-written with Tom Marcoux and various contributors)
* Endorsed by marketing expert Jay Conrad Levinson,
author of *Guerilla Marketing* series of books

Weigh Less Express:
From BIG Butts to Going Gangbusters:
Six Single Steps to Residual Eating

Marry Your Self First:
Your Key to Manifesting Loving Relationships
(also available as an ebook)

Dedication

I dedicate this book to all the amazing stylists who worked for me over my fourteen years of salon ownership. I am grateful to them for their expertise, loyalty, commitment and professionalism.

Acknowledgments

I would like to thank my first edit artist, Sandy Holt for her good work. Big thanks to salesmen Rich Karner and Bob Polizotto for years of kindness and guidance. Many thanks to Trudi McKamey, Linda Teets, and Lynn Crostreet for their love and support. More appreciation and hugs to my mother Tillie and sister Paula for their love and assistance throughout the years.

Table of Contents

CHAPTER ONE
The BIGGEST Secret of All! 1

It's All About the Client! 1
How to Meet the Salon Ownership Challenge 4
The Characteristics of a Star Enterprise....................................4

CHAPTER TWO
Make it BIG with Salon Ownership 7

Your General Start-up Costs 8
How Much Money Can You Expect to Make? 10
Ten BIG Advantages of Owning a Professional Salon...............14
The Disadvantages of Owning a Professional Salon.................16

CHAPTER THREE
Goals: Your Blueprint for Success 19

Define Your Purpose 19
Transforming Your Goal into Reality.......................................21
Win BIG by Setting Priorities 30

CHAPTER FOUR
Identify Your Business..33

Become a Specialist...33
Choose a Legal Form 34
Eight Ways to Finance Your New Salon...................................47

CHAPTER FIVE
Identify Your Competition...51

Know Who You're Up Against: Eleven Critical Questions 52

CHAPTER SIX
How to Develop a Winning Business Plan 57

The Three Functions of a Business Plan....................................... 57
A Tool for Bankers and Venture Capitalists 59
Business Plan Components.. 61
Definition of the Business... 66
Income Potential... 67
Promotion and Advertising Plan 70

CHAPTER SEVEN
Your Legal Responsibilities 77

Your State Board License 77
Tax Deductions, Knowing the Law.. 78
Business Use of Home... 79
Regulations, Business Laws and Insurance Regulations........... 82

CHAPTER EIGHT
Bookkeeping Made Easy 85

Managing Payroll... 87
Start-up Costs Worksheet 88
Monthly Business Expense 89
Cash Flow Forecast 90
Accounting and Control.. 92
Automation: Choose Your Computer.. 93

CHAPTER NINE
Cash in on Other People's Expertise 97

Solo, but not Alone.. 98
Create Your Own Support Team 98
Where to Look for Business Advisors.. 99
Win BIG with Credit 104

CHAPTER TEN
How to Develop a Grand Salon Image 107

Design Your Image for Your Specific Market........................... 108
How to Create a Positive Personal Image 110
Develop Outstanding Management Skills 112
Twelve Ways to Protect Your Image 113
How to Discover Trends 117
Demographic Profile and Trends 119

CHAPTER ELEVEN
Make it BIG With the Right Location 121

How to Find the Perfect Location 121
The Advantage of Owning Your Own Property 123
Negotiating a Lease: Buyer Beware 124

CHAPTER TWELVE
How to Design Your New Salon 129

Create a Winning Business Name.. 129
Evaluate Your Present Space.. 132
The In's and Out's of Buying Equipment................................ 133
How to Purchase Inexpensive Equipment 135
How to Maximize Profits in Your Reception Area..................... 140
Make Big Profits From Your Retail Area 141
How to Set up the Styling Area.. 143
Remodel Your Secondhand Salon 149

CHAPTER THIRTEEN
Standard and Complimentary Services 155

Choosing Right Services.. 155
Influence Clients with Apparel and Boutique Items.................. 158
Innovate with Computer Imaging 160
Start a Wig Center 165
The Benefits of an Ear Piercing Center 165
Hair Accessories as a Profit Maker 166
Be HOT Stuff: a Tanning Bed or Booth 166
Stimulate New Business with Workshops or Open Houses 167
Make BIG Money with Massage and Spa Treatments 168
Esthetics as a Profit Center 169
Day Spa Services.. 169
Create a Beauty Supply Center for BIG profits........................ 170
Open a Beauty School 173

CHAPTER FOURTEEN
How to Price Your Services 175

Set Your Fee Structure 175
Raise Your Prices 176
What to Charge Family and Friends 177
Check Cashing Policies and Credit Cards.................. 178

CHAPTER FIFTEEN
Make it BIG with the Best Employees 181

How to Choose the Right Employees........................... 183
Eight Steps to the Hiring Process............................... 184
Seek Useful Skills.. 187
Application Form 190
Find the Secret to Motivating Employees 193
Employee Classifications.. 199
The Scoop on Independent Contractors 200
Hire a Salon Coordinator, Receptionist, or Manager.................... 201
Three Critical Characteristics of the Salon Coordinator 203
Make it BIG With a Manicurist or Nail Technician 208
Make it BIG With an Esthetician 209
Motivate Your Way to Success 211
Educate Your Staff about Products 221

CHAPTER SIXTEEN
Maximize Salon Potential 223

How to Keep Your Clients.. 224
Ensure Salon Success: Fourteen Guidelines............... 225
Avoid a Dysfunctional Workplace................................ 229

CHAPTER SEVENTEEN
Optimize Retail Sales..233

Retail Profitability... 233
How Revealing Your Clientele Can Also Boost Retail Sales.................. 235
The 7 Principles of Great Retailing.. 239
Predicting Retail Sales 242
How to Price Your Products 243
How to Choose Between Brand Name and Private Label Products........... 244
Retail Questionnaire 248
Teach Employees How to Sell.. 249

CHAPTER EIGHTEEN
Market Your Salon for BIG Success 255

Ten Steps to Better Marketing.. 255
Network Marketing - Build a Network of Allies................................ 264
Do It Yourself Graphic Design.. 266
The Rules for Effective Advertising... 272
Internet Marketing... 276
Search Engine Optimization (SEO) 281
Social Media... 284
How to Change Direction When Necessary 292

CHAPTER NINETEEN
Quitting Your Business..295

Cut the Cord... 295
How to Sell Your Salon 296

Introduction

Hair salons and small businesses alike have been failing at an alarming rate. In 1992, there were 160,000 hair salons across the nation. Now there are barely 74,000 still in existence. Actually, that's good news for salon owners who have the good fortune to still be in business. They have much less competition for clients. Yet the statistics are less than admirable for those other 86,000 salon owners whose hopes and dreams were riding on business success. Nor are these figures inspiring for students and entrepreneurs who would someday love to try their luck in the salon business. The point is it's not necessarily luck that makes one entrepreneur more successful than another. The difference between a successful salon owner and a former salon owner who had a bad experience is a smart decision making process. An uninformed person cannot make intelligent decisions until he or she has the correct and appropriate resource information. Only then can one reach the pinnacle of success in any industry.

This information is an honest, tried and true resource to help you make those critical decisions. It can take you from being a dreamer or a wanna be salon owner to a proud, successful salon entrepreneur.

I help solve the problem of potential salon owners who want to be a part of the exciting and lucrative salon business, but who lack the necessary skills. Benefit from first hand experience. Learn everything you didn't learn in beauty school ... all the real world experience.

Many hair stylists are creative, but not business-minded. Beauty school provides a beneficial process for developing technical skills, but minimal training for the challenge of salon ownership. You'll find blueprints, checklists, exercises, forms, tips and more to shorten your learning curve.

My goal is to assist you in the decision-making process so you may become as prosperous as you desire to be. You'll learn to prevent costly errors, and avoid problematic situations. I expose you to the facts as I understand them to be. I lead you through the intricate maze of business ownership.

This publication answers the one main question, "How do I manifest the successful salon of my dreams?"

Learn from the successes and mistakes of others. If this knowledge saves you from becoming one more statistic, then it has achieved its goal.

A successful salon can provide you with a vast array of worldly benefits: prestige, financial independence, a luxurious home, nice cars, exotic travel opportunities and many more desirable material comforts. I know because I had them all. While numerous perks of the trade are certainly a grand enticement, they are not exclusively reason enough to start a salon business. You must want to offer something unique or different. Those who have achieved success in this business know that it must be in your blood, and you must be passionate about it.

For the Budding Entrepreneur

As an entrepreneur who is examining various businesses in which to invest, you'll learn the nitty gritty of salon life. You'll learn the advantages and disadvantages of the salon business.

After serving nine years as a hairstylist, I opened my first salon in 1975 with very little knowledge of business principles, so I know first hand the difficulties and complexities of business ownership. For me it was a mixed experience, by that I mean one of great joy as well as a few sorrows. To look at the statistics and reasons for small business failure, I realize I was not the only entrepreneur who felt sorrowful from time to time. Owning your own business can be either a happy, growth experience or it can be your worst nightmare.

I believe that most of the failures and nightmares, if not all, can be avoided in the first place by having enough of the right kind of guidance and information at your fingertips. When I sold my salon, I realized that I had become a much more wise and adept business person. My mission is to share with you the knowledge I gained from this rewarding and fulfilling experience. You too can express yourself creatively, have fun, and be a prosperous salon owner/entrepreneur.

Your Formula for Success

Throughout the years, I studied the most successful entrepreneurs, and the well-known movers and shakers. It became clear to me that there is a well-defined formula for success. While each individual contains within themselves various admirable qualities, there are certain ingredients that contribute greatly to business prosperity. The conscientious entrepreneur must first of all be a humanitarian by nature. He or she has integrity, sincerity, honesty and gives without thought of return. You stir all that up then add an authentic dedication to quality and creativity, and a sincere commitment to professionalism. Last but not least, include your own unique personality, and you have an award winning formula for success.

Many of the topics are directed toward first time salon owners, but most of the information will apply to experienced salon owners as well. They'll help you make it BIG in the hair salon business. Be sure not to skip over anything. Little pearls of wisdom are included with most topics. Some information may not be relevant to you now, but may become so in the future as new developments occur within your salon. May all your hopes and dreams come true.

Foreword

This publication is not meant to be all-inclusive, nor the last word on anything. Good decision-making always requires common sense and intuition.

CHAPTER ONE
The BIGGEST Secret of All!

It's All About the Client!

May I be the first to burst your bubble? The salon business or any business is not about you. I know you have goals and dreams and they are important to you. You've worked your tail off and saved a bunch of money to establish your first salon business. You're smart, talented, creative, and have everything going for you. Trained and creative staff are waiting to follow you. You prepared yourself with management, sales and marketing skills. Guess what? It's still not about you. Nor is it about your ego. It's not about the salon design, expensive top of the line equipment, or your dynamic looking logo. Those are all nice accruements to attract clients to your new or current salon, but they may not be the real reason clients come to you. It's all about the client!

Clients may come to you because you consider yourself the best stylist, haircutter or colorist in your geographical area. You may not be the best, but maybe they just like you or they like someone who works for you. You may be in a convenient location, or your low prices may be attractive. You may be the new kid on the block that everyone is talking about. Clients have lots of personal reasons to go to a certain salon or leave it behind. You are in business for two reasons ... to serve the client's needs and to get them to return. It's about them and if you always remember that and make whatever you do in your business about them, you should do pretty well. This book is about setting everything up to attract and keep the ideal client. You must still do your part and let it also be about living your dream, even if it's not totally about you.

Remember that every client is not there for you. They are there for themselves. Whatever you offer to sell them: services or products, the one question that is always in the back of their mind is, "What's in it for me?" If you can honestly answer that one question *through benefits to the client* then you are in good shape. You are wasting your time and energy if there is no personal benefit to that client. Neither will they return.

There are three things people want: they want to be wanted, recognized, and appreciated. If you help them with those unspoken goals, you'll probably do pretty well. You and your employees have the opportunity to provide these basic needs and more to the general public.

You have the power of touch. You touch people physically and you touch them emotionally. You can make a difference in someone's life by helping them look and feel good about themselves and you don't even have to say a word. There are not many careers paths that can make that claim. Working with the general public can be fun and it can also be difficult, but if you keep in mind what they are there for (other than a service) you will do pretty well, if not amazing.

Who is Your Client?

This is the one main question you will need to answer for yourself before you open or can continue your business. Of all the information I give you in this book I can't tell you who your client or clients are. That's something you must discern for yourself. What I can do is guide you through the process of elimination or discovery. Through inquiry you may be able to answer this critical question. All the other information offered can help you attract and win over that client.

Tip: You will find more information on your target market in *"Chapter Eighteen: Marketing Your Salon for BIG Success."*

Exercise:
In order to pinpoint your target market, please respond to the following questions:

1. What do you do that is unique or special?

2. Create a profile of your 'best' client (who would want what you offer):

3. Write a descriptive analysis of who your *current* clients are:

4. Write a descriptive analysis of who your *potential* clients are. Include each of your target markets.

    A. Target Market No. 1
    What are their interests, lifestyle factors, and where you can find them?

    B. Target Market No. 2
    What are their interests, lifestyle factors, and where you can find them?

5. How will you find the target market that wants what you have to offer?

How to Meet the Salon Ownership Challenge

The salon business is a people-oriented business, which means that your commitment will be continuously challenged. Be firm in your commitment to override those inevitable bumps in the road. Meet the salon ownership challenge by developing six management and entrepreneurial strengths: enthusiasm, knowledge, planning, action, listening and commitment. But the real basis of this formula is commitment. Without a commitment, the other five strengths dissolve away.

This book is designed to cut short the learning curve of starting, owning and operating a successful hair salon. A successful client relationship depends on your ability to run your business effectively.

The Characteristics of a Star Enterprise

1. Enthusiasm
You must ask yourself one critical question about your commitment to making it BIG in this industry, "are you excited by it?" Do you wake up in the morning and look forward to another busy, lucrative day in the salon helping clients look their best? Add a double dose of enthusiasm to a successful formula and you have the option of *surpassing* your predecessors.

2. Knowledge
You've probably heard the old adage "knowledge is power?" What you know that other people don't can be one of your top strengths. That's why I encourage new business owners to stay abreast of what's going on in their industry as well as other industries. You can learn from everyone.

This book is an important resource and will provide you with the necessary *knowledge* you need to succeed in this lucrative industry. I worked in the cosmetology profession as a salon owner and/or as a stylist for over thirty years. I began my tenure first as a stylist, then as salon owner very much like you. I had very little training and a lot of high aspirations. I took one step at a time, educated myself and then built salons that made me proud.

3. Planning

The best possible outcomes don't happen by chance. They are carefully laid plans that happen on purpose. If you truly care about making it BIG in the salon business, you must *plan* to make it BIG. This book is the result of many years of research, study, and experimentation. Each step in the process will help you to plan your strategies in an effective way to take your salon business to the next level of success.

4. Action

Making it BIG in this industry is the result of acting in a BIG way. Every effort has been made to inspire and motivate you into *action*. All of the most important knowledge in the world and the best made plans mean absolutely nothing unless you act on your decisions. Good intentions are admirable, but are laid to rest along with lost dreams.

5. Listen

As a stylist or salon owner the most important thing you can do every day is to listen. Let the word *listen* be a mantra to you. Don't talk, just listen. While your creative and technical skills are important, they are detrimental without good listening skills. Listen when your clients speak. Listen to each word they say when they describe what they want or what they don't want. Listen and remember what they say about the products you refer to them or sell them. Listen when they give you feedback about your work. Listen when they complain about something. They are doing you a favor and you must take it as such. It's your opportunity to make an improvement and you've gotten the feedback for free, unless they quit you. Listening will get you much farther in this business than chatting clients up all the time about this or that. Talk about something beneficial to the client. Talk about things that will improve their lives, inspire them or make them laugh. They also listen carefully to you. You are the respected and trustworthy professional. What you say about services and products matters to them, as it should. Speak intelligently, listen and follow through and you'll build a loyal and trusting clientele.

6. Commitment

Examine your commitment level before you make any steps toward salon ownership. Where are you on a scale of one to ten, with one being the least amount of commitment and ten being the highest amount of commitment toward salon ownership? Opening a business is a big step, not to be taken lightly. There's a big financial and personal risk. Read this book first, then assess whether you have what it takes to run a hair salon everyday. Are you mature and reliable enough to take on the responsibilities of employees who depend on you for a paycheck, and clients who depend on you to have a stable, safe and viable business?

Tip: No one can *guarantee* another person's success. But by following in the footsteps of successful people before you, your chances of attaining a comparable degree of accomplishment is much greater.

In Conclusion

This critical first chapter helps you understand that the client is your most important mirror or feedback mechanism for how well or how poorly you are doing in your business. Learn what your strengths and weaknesses are, so you can show off your strengths and replace weaknesses with additional training.

CHAPTER TWO
Make it BIG with Salon Ownership

Let's imagine you are ready to open your first salon, and you want to make it BIG. You've been out of beauty school for a while, and gained experience by working for someone else. Or perhaps you're an entrepreneur who is excited about the salon industry and wants to get in on the action. In either case, you're certain that you have something unique to offer your community that isn't already being provided. You have the potential to make it BIG. One necessary element to making it BIG is having enough money to open a business. What's great about a salon business is that it doesn't cost much money to open a small *mom and pop* salon. So you ask the first important question, "How much is a salon going to cost me?"

Start-up Expenses

Start-up expenses will vary. The amount of money you'll need depends upon whether you start from scratch, purchase an existing salon or go with a franchise operation. (See *Chapter Four: Identify Your Business* for franchise information.)

Today the average price for a start-up salon is at least $25,000.00 or more depending upon the quantity and quality of new or used equipment you purchase and the image you want to project.

I opened my first salon in 1975 on a shoestring as so many stylist/owners do. After renting an inexpensive mall location in my small town, I added plumbing, electrical, and a little decor. A local beauty supply house allowed me to purchase three workstations on consignment, and some new pieces of equipment. I acquired the balance of my inexpensive equipment at a garage sale from a disenchanted former salon owner. I ordered my products and tools, and within a short time I was in business for about $3,000. Many people are shocked when I tell them how I began. It just shows you what is possible when you want something bad enough. My second salon opened five years later in 1980. I bought the best equipment available and the decor was more elaborate. The completed salon that I was so proud of cost me about $35,000.00. So you see, there can be a substantial price difference.

Your General Start-up Costs

Rent .... $700-1,500 per month & up

Inventory and supplies .... $3,000-5,000 to start

New equipment...$20,000+

Used equipment..$5,000+

Leasehold improvements...$10,000+

Licenses and fees.. $50-150+

Advertising and Promotion.....................................$1,000 and up

Utility and phone deposit................................. $200-300 and up

Office Supplies and File Cabinet............................ $200 and up

Accounting and legal Services .... $300-500 and up

Insurance ....$2000+ per quarter

* These figures are minimal and not all-inclusive. Prices will vary according to the elaborate nature of your business. The choice of a suburban or city location, and the section of the country in which you open will also have an effect upon your cost factor.

Choose the Right Equipment

Go to your local beauty supply house and price its in-house equipment or look through catalogs to view current styles. Your salesperson and a manufacturers' representative will help you to choose your new equipment. You can also view and price new equipment at larger trade shows.

Used equipment can be found in the classified ads or at auctions or garage sales. Make sure everything works before you buy. You can find fabulous buys at an auction if you're not particular about your choice of furnishings. Antiques set a nice mood for a more unique and individualized approach to decorating. Be creative. It's fun and will set you apart from other salons.

Equipment list and costs:
- Reception desk and chair   _____
- Hydraulic chairs   _____
- Styling stations   _____
- Back bar and sinks   _____
- Shampoo chairs   _____
- Other   _____

Booth Rental

Booth rental is great if you merely want to be self-employed, and not have employees. You will still have responsibilities since it is your salon. Choose renters wisely and make certain they are licensed. You'll determine a fair rental price, establish some rules and policies, and collect rent. These people are using your name so make certain they represent you well.

Another option is to rent a booth from a nearby salon. Booth prices will vary depending upon the salon's overhead. The going price at this writing is around $500 per month, depending on many factors. This is a fairly efficient way to become self-employed without having to deal with your own employees. Of course you don't get the additional income. You and the other principals must determine how walk-in clients will be distributed, along with other major decisions pertaining to salon care, advertising, retail sales, telephone, business hours, etc.

How Much Money Can You Expect to Make?

Actually there is no limit to what you can make. The amount of revenue you can generate depends upon many variables: your location, size of salon, your price point, stylist's capabilities, competition, and your own ingenuity. I know of several one-person home salons that make about $15,000 a year or more. A larger commercial salon can gross anywhere from $100,000 to $300,000 or more per year. Don't set your goals too high for the first year or two, as it takes time to establish a good reputation in the community. Your business will build up as satisfied clients tell their friends. Expect typical revenues to expand at least 10-25% each year.

I have found that female clients, on the average, spend between $20.00 and $35.00 per salon visit, not including the average retail expenditure of about $15-20.00. If you already have a clientele, you can roughly estimate how much revenue they'll be bringing to your new salon. Then add your potential market, and you should have a good idea of your revenue.

Secret: I found that it takes about two years before a salon really gets going.

A Start-Up Checklist For Your New Salon

√ Choose a name and an image. Write a business plan.
√ Find a suitable location.

√ Choose an attorney and an accountant.

√ Open a bank account and get a DBA (doing business as).

√ Negotiate a lease.

√ Get a Federal tax number and send for state sales tax number.

√ Advertise for employees.

√ Develop a floor plan, choose equipment, and a sign.

√ Write to your state board for a license.

√ Hire your contractor or carpenters, plumbers, electricians, painters etc. Complexity of   design and construction will determine length of time before you open your doors to the public. Plan on at least a month or two.

√ Put deposits on your utilities and garbage service.

√ Talk to a graphic designer about your image and what promotional materials you might need. Order business cards, receipt books, application forms, retail shopping bags, promotional flyers and rubber stamps.

√ Purchase products, working tools, office supplies and refreshment supplies.

√ Purchase advertising and set up an open house.

√ Relax and have fun.

Are *You* an Entrepreneur?

Owning your own business is truly the *American Dream*. Many have found that the fantasy can often times be much more appealing than the reality. Before you get caught up in all of the glamorous aspects of entrepreneurship, you must find out if the shoe fits. By that I mean you must thoroughly research what is required of you before you act.

When looking at an attractive new pair of shoes, you must determine if these particular shoes are the best and most intelligent choice. As we all have learned through experience, new leather shoes are very defined, so your feet must be a perfect size for the fit to be comfortable. Entrepreneurship follows a similar concept.

Studies have been done on the topic of what successful people *do* to become successful and to *maintain* a high level of accomplishment. It has been found that they all have similar qualities, habits, and ways of thinking which contribute to their overall success.

They have an extraordinary need to achieve. They are driven by their inventiveness and follow through with their plans. A positive attitude is natural for them, and they radiate that attitude to those around them until everyone is inspired by it. Entrepreneurs are positive thinkers who have the unlimited energy to find a better way. They have a healthy respect for money. Their oral and written communication skills serve them to become respected and admired. They understand the value of human resources and treat everyone they meet with honesty and integrity.

Sincerely study your self and your abilities to determine if you have the qualifications to fit into these clearly defined shoes. Whenever these shoes do fit properly, they will take you through the door of opportunity provided by the professional salon business.

Exercise: What motivates you to want your own salon business?

Salon Ownership and Entrepreneurship

I feel that just about anyone can own a professional hair salon. It isn't necessary to be a licensed cosmetologist to own a salon, however, you'll need a licensed cosmetologist working for you who does have a manager's license. You'll need to check with your state board laws for specific information regarding licenses and regulations. Basically what you'll need is knowledge of business principles: bookkeeping, business laws, insurance, marketing, salesmanship, and psychology. You'll also need a sense of dedication.

There are many critical decisions to be made before starting a salon business. The first and most important decision is whether you desire *to be or not to be* an independent business owner. This information will help you ascertain whether you want to remain behind the chair working as a stylist or go the entrepreneurial route by taking on responsibilities and opening a business enterprise.

There is always a large risk involved: your money, your emotional well-being, your self-esteem, and your personal reputation. You are gambling against the odds, and statistically the odds are against you. You can shift the odds in your favor by learning business principles and having enough cash flow on hand.

Apprenticeship Training as a Career Advantage

You may play it safe and easy by working for someone else for a while as an apprentice. In fact, I recommend that you work for someone else until you build up financial reserves and learn business savvy. Serving an apprenticeship can be a valuable experience if the business owner you serve with is truly a good leader. If not, learning poor leadership skills in the beginning could undermine your own learning process.

You'll then need to do your own footwork and prepare yourself for the future. It is important to observe and learn from the mistakes and successes of others. Business ownership is not to be taken lightly. It is a major decision, which will bring about dramatic changes in your life and to those around you: family, friends, and acquaintances. Its far-reaching effects will influence people you haven't even met yet. When you feel competent and ready for self-employment, you can forge ahead with confidence.

Increase Effectiveness Through Absentee Ownership

You can also be an absentee owner, but you'll need a full time manager to manage your business for you. Be certain that person is well-trained, or they could do more harm than good. If you should decide to open a chain of salons, as so many entrepreneurs are now doing, you will need more free time to effectively manage them all.

Ten BIG Advantages of Owning a Professional Salon

1. You can make a cash investment. A small start-up could cost you very little for a home-based or small salon, to as much as $25,000 or more. It all depends upon the quality of equipment you purchase and the image you want to project.

2. The salon business is recession proof. Everyone at one time or another needs professional salon services. Even in the worst of times people want to look good and feel good about themselves. Many women especially, will cut down on other purchases such as clothes and dining out so they can afford to be personally groomed at a professional salon.

3. You can be an absentee owner, but you'll need a qualified manager who is effective enough to handle your salon business for you. Your success or failure will be in your manager's hands, so be sure you investigate this person's credentials, honesty, and integrity before you make a hiring decision. If you have previous business experience, you will have more control over the situation.

4. It's a stable industry. There will always be a need for good

14

professional hair salons. Even people who don't use your hair services may have a need for retail products, manicures, nail treatments, tanning or other services. Your business will appeal to a larger audience if you offer a wide range of services.

5. There is a risk factor. There is always a certain amount of risk in any business venture. Good business skills, capable employees and a good location will increase your chances of success. A knowledgeable business consultant can help if you have any concerns or doubts about a particular decision.

6. The salon business provides you with the potential to have a flexible schedule. You can set your own hours to have more time with your family, take vacations, or pursue other interests.

7. Independence is certainly one vital benefit of salon ownership. You are your own boss, and can make the decisions which you feel will support and benefit your salon.

8. You will experience increased personal satisfaction. Business ownership is a growth experience and will allow you to feel a sense of pride and accomplishment.

9. You have the opportunity to serve the community by contributing to the welfare of employees and clients. It gives one a sense of humanitarianism when your efforts are well-received.

10. Possibly the best advantage of all is that the salon industry is a fascinating outlet for creative-minded, enthusiastic individuals. This exciting field is never boring or inhibitive. It's an extremely rewarding field for entrepreneurs who are truly people-oriented.

The Disadvantages of Owning a Professional Salon

1. Current studies determine that two out of five new small businesses survive at least six years. The statistics may appear depressing and can be cause for concern. The two major reasons most businesses fail are *mismanagement* and *under capitalization*.

2. One major disadvantage of the salon business, as in many businesses, is that it can take as long as two years or more before you see your business really taking off. The profit margin may be slow in the beginning. The exception would be if you opened your salon with several stylists who have their own large clientele.

3. For many years, the salon industry has been attracting a part-time work force, which slows productivity. The cost of overhead is extremely high, so each chair must bring in a certain amount of revenue to cover the cost per square foot of rental space. It is often difficult to fill the empty chair of a part time employee. If the chair is taken by a part-timer on the traditionally busy days of Thursday through Saturday, then you must find an employee who is willing to work the slower days. In order to make the chair profitable that employee must retain clients who prefer the Sunday or Monday through Wednesday shift.

In another scenario you may have a part-timer who can only work certain hours, perhaps 10:00 am to 3:00 pm on Monday through Friday due to family obligations. While the hours before 10:00 am and after 3:00 pm are potentially profitable, you may have difficulty finding someone willing to work a split shift.

4. Another disadvantage are the long hours, perhaps ten to fourteen hours per day, six or seven days per week. As

the business owner you may still be working behind the chair with a large clientele while actively promoting your salon, and taking care of the operational end of the business.

5. You must assess the financial risks. A large investment in a prestigious rental unit and upscale equipment does not guarantee success.

Exercise:
List your strength and weaknesses. What are the advantages and/or disadvantages of salon ownership that stand out for you?

In Conclusion
You can make BIG money with salon ownership when you are able to keep tab on your costs. There are advantages and disadvantages that should be taken into account before you decide on ownership. Spend time thinking about your leadership skills, character, business skills, temperament, and ability to communicate effectively with others.

Notes:

CHAPTER THREE
Goals: Your Blueprint for Success

What does it mean to you to *Make it BIG in the Hair Salon Business?*

Every entrepreneur will have their own idea of what making it BIG means. Having a clear and concise vision for your business can drive you toward success. Let it be a vision that is realistic and attainable. You must establish it to yourself first, then find others interested in helping you manifest it.

Define Your Purpose

You should have a clear idea of your purpose and why you are starting your own business. Get clear about this in the beginning and remember that it isn't written in stone. You can be flexible if you find your initial purpose did not prove fruitful. Use this exercise to become clear about your purpose.

Exercise:

1. Why are you in business or want to have your own business?

2. What do you plan to accomplish?

3. How do you plan to accomplish it?

4. What gives meaning to your life?

5. What direction are you going? (Remember, it's an ongoing process that you need not complete.)

6. What are your values?

Create a BIG Experience

Daydreams are valuable exercises in *creative imagining*. They help you create the situations and experiences you want to have in your life. The dreams or experiences may be to graduate from college, go to a trade school, or even start your own business. Many of the daydreams tend to be fantasies, but as a few catch on you become attached to them. Feel the passion and know those are the ones that are part of your life plan. It's important to dream BIG and create a BIG experience in your heart and mind. It's what will keep you moving forward when challenges arise.

Make time to think and dream about your future salon. Let it become a part of you, something that already exists in your head. Creating a BIG experience means bringing it out of your head and into the world through *baby steps*.

Some effort may be required (education, research, finances) to pursue your dreams. In the final round, you will choose and aim for only those experiences in which you are passionate. It is your passion that will motivate you to choose your most desired dreams and bring them to life. We call this process *setting goals*.

Tip: Dreams or goals are brought to life by giving them our *energy* and *enthusiasm*, which is essentially our passion. A goal cannot be accomplished without this main ingredient.

Transforming Your Goal into Reality

In order to win BIG, you must be able to think BIG.

1. Let go of limiting thoughts. Immediately correct any negative thoughts that tend to downplay your potential.

2. Have a grand vision for your salon. Be clear on what you want. Notice what everyone else is doing that is mundane or routine. Ask yourself what you can do that is better and will make an impact on your community?

3. Have a viable, concrete plan.

4. Study what other successful professionals are doing, and take action to follow in their footsteps, or surpass them.

The Manifestation of Goals

How your goals will manifest to you and to your community is a matter of your inner visualization and your commitment to its potential. You'll create an inner vision (the dream, experience, goal) in your mind of how you want the experience to be in reality. This is your starting point. As you think it through, and establish the details, you'll find that your ideas gain more clarity. By consciously reiterating the experience in your mind, you program yourself to become more aware of the goal and its implications. As your awareness increases, your conscious mind integrates the information and synchronistic events happen. This brings about circumstances that lead you to the next step or level of accomplishment. You must continue to perceive your goals in a positive light by keeping your inner vision constant in your mind.

You'll set your dreams in motion by doing two important things: giving them your energy and being enthusiastic about them. The goal transfers from an inner vision to outer reality by following these nine action steps.

Eight Action Steps to Achieve Your Goals

1. Listen to Your Heart

Commitment to the accomplishment of your salon owner-ship goal must come from your heart, not your ego. Current economic conditions may point out that careers in nursing or computer science are the wave of the future. That's not reason enough to pursue those vocations. If you don't have the dedication of a nurse or computer scientist, you won't be happy or be truly helpful in those professions. Whenever there is an obvious conflict in your mind about a goal, then it is time to re-evaluate the reasons you chose the goal in the first place. Perhaps it was just something you wished you could do, but you had no deep understanding of what effort would be required to accomplish it. Perhaps more detailed research would determine how passionate you are about your business goals.

2. Establish Personal Clarity

It is extremely important for you to *know yourself.* You need to be aware of your strengths and your weaknesses. You must make a realistic evaluation of your past behaviors and experiences. How can you improve upon them?

3. Put Your Goals in Writing

A goal is just a *thought* until you set it in motion through your actions. Writing your goals on paper reinforces them in your mind. It's like a road map that reminds you of your direction as well as your destination. Writing your goals on paper and sharing them with supportive people are two means for making your dreams a reality.

Once your goals are on paper, you must set a timeline, and decide what needs to be done this week, this month and in the next three to six months. You'll also find value in scheduling activities for the next year, three to five years and ten years.

4. Find a Mentor

Talking to someone you know who has attained a similar goal can help clarify matters. Gain valuable insight by learning how your predecessors solved their problems of getting started. How do they manage the daily start up challenges of hiring the right employees, or of choosing vendors such as real estate agents, plumbers and accountants? The SBA (Small Business Administration) has a team of volunteer and retired business people (SCORE) who offer to mentor you for free. Take advantage of their free counseling and classes.

5. Develop a Team

Most goals will require the input or effort of more than one person. Join a Mastermind group. This is a group of like-minded entrepreneurs who guide and coach each other towards their greatest potential.

You could hire a business coach to get you going and keep you on track. Let the coach know your comfort level with moving forward. A good one can help make dreams come true.

Improve your business by getting your employees involved. Work as a team to expand your services. Establish a family atmosphere by introducing your clients to other personnel in the salon. Studies have shown that clients who receive more than one service are more apt to become loyal followers than individuals who receive only one service.

6. Be Authentic

When goals do not become reality, you must step back and evaluate the reasons. Perhaps the goal is not authentically yours. Maybe it's something a parent or a mate wishes for you. If the passion isn't there, accomplishment of the goal will probably not be there either.

7. Develop Your Confidence

Does lack of confidence hold you back? You achieve clarity of your goal, and have all the elements of success, but don't forge ahead. You may perceive yourself as unworthy of success, or fear the changes that a successful life will certainly bring. These are all natural responses. Through counseling, you can gain knowledge and information about yourself, and that information may heal any previous negative conditioning.

8. Be Realistic

Keep your goal realistic. You may have visions of a grand salon, but lack the necessary ingredients to make it happen: money, support from family, business skills, and a client base. In this case it would be wise to wait until your situation changes. Continue to plan for your goal and develop needed skills, but hold off on any concrete action until the right opportunity arises.

Your Personal Adaptability Quiz

1. What things have you done successfully in your life?

2. What do you desire to do that will enhance your life?

3. What changes would you have to make to get what you want?

4. What actions are you willing to take to make these changes possible?

5. Do you get along with current co-workers and managers?

6. What things have you been praised for doing well?

7. What are some of the things you really like do?

8. Name some situations that you really like or dislike?

9. What do you think are your good points?

10. What do others think are your good points?

11. For what characteristics have previous employers praised you?

12. What mental barriers do you set up to prevent yourself from accomplishing what you desire to do?

13. What mental barriers do you need to work on for self-employment success?

14. Do you have a great need to be liked? Give an example of a time when you said or did something necessary without being concerned about your popularity.

15. Are you attached to being right every time? Give an example of a time when you let go of the need to be right and another time when you didn't.

16. Are you a self-starter? Can you do things on your own without someone telling you what to do? Give an example.

17. Do you get along well with other people?

18. Do you speak only when necessary?

19. Do you have a friendly personality and the ability to carry on a conversation with many different types of people? Give some examples.

20. Do you have an adaptable attitude? Give an example of a time when a situation looked dim, and then you had a positive shift in attitude.

21. Are you a leader, or do you prefer to sit back and let others lead? Give an example of a time when you took the lead.

22. Are you a responsible person, or do you just let things go? Give an example of a time when you chose to be responsible.

23. How good are your organization skills? Have you ever created a plan, and executed it to completion? Give an example.

24. Do you have a good work ethic and are you able to make your work a priority? Give an example.

25. Are you a good decision maker? Give an example of when a quick decision you made proved fortuitous.

26. You may be required to make snap decisions. High pressure salespeople will give you no more than 30 seconds to make a purchasing decision. These instances will require you to rely on previous experience, common sense, and good judgment. How will you handle a high pressure salesperson?

27. Can your employees and clients trust you on your word?

Give an example of a time when you made a statement from your heart and then followed through or didn't follow through? What was the result?

28. Can you finish what you start? Name a situation where you were scattered and one where you were focused? What were the results?

29. Are you healthy and energetic enough to be consistent in your efforts? What steps will you take to maintain your good health?

30. What can you do on a daily basis to free your mind of negative thoughts or negative self-talk that may block you from success?

31. Do your family and friends realize you will work more, spend more time at the salon, and less time with them? It may seem like a 24 hours a day job. How will you explain to loved ones about the extra time away from them?

32. How will your family react to more or less money than before?

Set Salon Goals

Goal-setting becomes effective when you are clear about what you want. Here are some questions that will help you become gain clarity about your new salon. Use your answers as a road-map to determine where you are now and how to get to your destination.

Exercise: It's time to be clear about what you want.

1. Where do you want to open your business? What city, state, or country?

2. Do you want multiple locations? If so, where?

3. What type of work location do you want: an in-home salon, a shopping center, or a free-standing unit?

4. How many hours per week do you want to work?

5. Do you want a partner or a group of partners? What would they do?

6. What is your ideal business atmosphere?

7. What is the ideal net profit each year?

8. What is your *after tax* salary requirement?

9. What benefits do you want your business to have (health insurance, paid vacations, bonuses and incentives, retirement plans)?

10. Who is your ideal client?

11. Which professions could provide referrals to your business?

12. For which professions could you be a source of referrals?

13. Describe the ideal business agreement. If you were the employee, what would you like your employer to offer?

14. What kind of products will you provide?

15. How much money will you spend on your marketing campaign each year?

Target Short Term Goals

If you want to make it BIG in the hair salon business, you must develop good planning habits. Create good habits by developing a goals list and making a commitment to follow through on the list.

Short term goals are goals that you intend to achieve immediately: for the day, the week, and the next three months. Make a list of the top six tasks you need to do tomorrow, then a list of tasks that need to be completed in a week, and another list for the forthcoming month. You may accomplish short term goals by finding financing to open your first salon. Make that call now.

An aggressive marketing campaign requires extensive research. Go to your local bookstore this week and buy a book on marketing, or promotion and advertising. What promotions will you do this month? Next month?

Do you need to increase your staff? Write a list of qualifications today, and tomorrow you will be ready to place your newspaper advertisement or internet posting.

You could research a new product line, perhaps even a private label line.

One Short term goal would be to develop all employees to their fullest potential. Example: send your shampoo person to school to learn nail care. Implement a computer and teach everyone the new software.

Exercise: Write down your short term goals for tomorrow, next week, next month, and for the next three months.

Create Long Term Goals

Long term goals are those that may be accomplished in the next year, five years or ten years. For example, you may want to expand your main salon or develop a chain of salons. Review your vision and business plan, and then realistically pinpoint the goals you want to accomplish within the next ten years. Make out a timeline where you will identify how much revenue you need to acquire.

The benefit in having long term goals is that it keeps you focused and engaged in your business for the long term. At some point you may become bored with the status quo. That's a good time to look at your plan and take the next step.

"Develop your own stylist training program. This assures that your stylists are receiving the education and knowledge to stay current in their skills."

Extra services can be added: tanning booths, facial services, a fashion boutique, beauty school, a beauty school or computer imaging. You will find more detailed information in *Chapter Thirteen: Standard and Complimentary Services.*

Team up with stylists when they are ready to go out on their own and become salon owners. Develop a partnership program with them by helping out with financing and start-up costs. You'll still receive part of the profits. You don't want your former employee to take business away and become a competitor, so you might as well face the facts and share your successes. It could be beneficial to both parties.

Win BIG by Setting Priorities

Once your goals and purpose are established, it is necessary to set priorities and take action. Establish the most important steps and focus on them first. The first step in setting up a business is usually the business plan. It helps you get clarity on your financials, skill set, analysis of target market and competition, and marketing plan. Look at *Chapter Six: How to Develop a Winning Business Plan.*

You know what needs to be done, and some of those needs are more important than others. Some may be time specific like setting up a checking account, speaking to an attorney, choosing equipment or deciding on key employees. Other duties such as buying towels, setting up displays, or arranging the supply room can be done at a later time, closer to opening. In fact you can delegate many of these tasks.

Make a list of your most important duties. Decide what needs to be done first, second, thirdly etc.

"The duties you choose immediately will be the duties that are of the most value to you."

For example, you may prefer to locate your salon in a specific neighborhood. The time you spend researching, speaking with realtors, and studying the demographics of the area will ascertain how significant a priority your location is to your success.

As you study your priority list, determine what chores can be delegated to someone else so you may have more free time to spend with the most pressing issues. A time management system will be most important to you when you are opening an additional salon or a series of salons and already have more than enough to do. Perhaps your salon coordinator could relieve you of some of the less important duties. There are many good time management books available at your local bookstore.

Exercise: Make a list of priorities

Forge Your Path

Knowing the steps and strategies to implement a successful business enterprise is beneficial, but all the knowledge in the world won't make your business successful unless you *follow through*. That is where the power lies.

In Conclusion

Establishing your purpose and goals help you gain clarity and make it easier to move forward. You set up each step of the way and follow through.

Notes:

CHAPTER FOUR
Identify Your Business

In order to *Make it BIG in the Salon Business,* your first most critical decision is to determine whether you want to make it BIG by yourself, with a partner, or within a corporate structure. The rule of thumb here is to look at your vision to determine which business form will support your dreams and goals. Remember that you can eventually change business forms if you find it necessary.

You must define to yourself, your employees, and the public what your business looks like. In defining the specifics of your particular business, you will use the knowledge gained from previous salon experience or a similar business environment. Both experience and research equal the knowledge and power needed to engage in an accurately defined profession.

Become a Specialist

There was a time when many medical doctors were considered general practitioners or G.P.'s. There were very few specialists. More doctors became specialists in order to stand out from the crowd and to survive financially.

For example, when a doctor or a lawyer opens their practice, they do not just open their doors one day and wait to see who drops in. They define their plan from the start and advertise accordingly. They educate themselves in all aspects of business ownership, perhaps serve an internship, then choose to become self-employed. A doctor will decide at the start if he is a general practitioner or if he is going to specialize in a particular area of medicine: a cardiologist, an osteopath, a diet doctor, an anesthesiologist or other type of specialist. Before he puts up a sign, he determines his specialty.

A lawyer will determine if he is a Patent, Trademark & Copyright attorney, a malpractice attorney, mediation, personal injury & property damage, corporate, criminal law or another.

You too, must also determine who you will be in the mind of the consumer. Will they think of your salon only when they need a quick haircut, or will they think of you when they desire to spend a full day being pampered? Your name may come to mind when the children need haircuts, but not the adults. The public may think of you just for the convenience of purchasing personal beauty supplies. Determine how you wish to be perceived by the public from the beginning, then do your best to play that role.

Choose a Legal Form

In this chapter you will seek to identify a legal business form. You'll answer the question of ownership. Do you have the abilities and strengths to go it alone and maintain a sole proprietorship, or do you need the assistance of one or more persons in order to be effective? You may choose a corporate structure in order to keep the business as a separate entity. Examine all the possibilities before you make this critical business decision.

There are three business forms from which to choose. The first is a sole proprietor, the second is a partnership, and the third is a corporation. Which one you choose depends on your business and personal goals. Each legal form will have its advantages and disadvantages. To make it clear you must state your goals and purpose, as well as your strengths and weaknesses. Your skills and your financial position may play a large part in your decision. Here are the various legal forms from which you will choose.

Become a Sole Proprietor

A sole proprietorship is one in which you are the only one who owns the business. It has the advantage of being the easiest form of business to start with limited funds. Usually a sole proprietorship is appropriate for a small to medium size salon.

You have the satisfaction of working for yourself, making all the decisions and having all the responsibility. You'll get all the profits and take all the losses. It is always the best way to go if you have the money and the expertise.

Self-employed people are permitted to set up retirement accounts for themselves and their employees. You will be able to bank some of your earnings for your own pension or IRA without having to pay income tax on that money until you begin to draw on it for income. At that time you will probably be in a much lower tax bracket.

There are also some disadvantages. Most businesses owned by one person tend to be small in size and in profits. The prosperity of the business depends upon the talents and managerial skills of one person. A sole proprietor often has difficulty borrowing money from the bank and frequently must pay higher interest rates.

There is also unlimited liability. Any damages or debt that can be attributed to the salon can be attached to the owner's personal assets. You might have enough insurance to cover public liability and malpractice, etc., and if your business is failing and your debt is high, your options are either to sell or file bankruptcy. If you can't sell, then your personal assets will be in danger.

Partnerships, a Joint Venture

A partnership is when two or more people agree to start or buy a business together.

Partnership advantages:

1. More money is available.

2. You can share skills, responsibilities, decisions, and expertise.

3. Each partner has a direct interest in the success of the business. If you decide to open more than one salon, you will have assistance and moral support.

4. Partnerships generally have higher credit ratings for the simple reason that the partners have unlimited personal liability for debts incurred by the partnership.

5. Partners, like sole proprietors, are taxed only on their personal incomes.

6. Having a partner can be advantageous during times when you run out of ideas, need time off, or just need to talk to someone who understands what the business is all about.

7. Having the good resources of a partner may make the difference between not starting at all or having your dream come true.

Finding and choosing a partner or partners can be a difficult process in itself. It requires considerable thought and self-assessment from both parties. Determine which resources you can both contribute and what roles you will play. Come to a conclusion about who will make important decisions and resolve conflicts.

It is advantageous in the start-up phases to have a mentor, someone with business experience and no investment in your business. Both you and your partner can bring problems and solutions to this person and expect fair advice.

Tip: The best partner is one whose talents compliment your own, but whose business philosophy, personality, and background differ. Your combined abilities give depth to the enterprise. Differing backgrounds act as a buffer against excesses of any kind.

There are also disadvantages of a partnership.

1. All the profits must be shared.

2. Each partner assumes the other's unlimited liability for debt. Many friendships have been ruined by business partnerships. Be particular about choosing a partner since many fail. You need someone who has these qualities: fair, honest, communicates well, is committed and willing to go the distance.

3. Another major disadvantage is the practical limit on the number of managing partners. Too many partners making decisions can contribute to ineffective management.

Be aware of which ideas you have in common and those areas which may present a potential conflict. It could be advantageous to provide a dissolution or buyout agreement. It is best to then have an attorney or business consultant review your plans, goals, and agreements and call attention to any potential conflicts.

Both parties may be starting out fresh and it will be a learning experience for both of you. Communication is critical in the beginning stages. Be sure each party expresses their goals and desires, the other understands them and is willing to work toward meeting those goals.

For example, two investors may bring together years of experience and an expanded clientele into one grand salon in order to compete for a larger share of the market. Another option is when a hair salon and a nail salon come together in a joint venture. Two hair salons with complimentary employees and clients may find it advantageous to join forces. Products bought in large quantities are less expensive. If this scenario appeals to you, then you will need to discuss fee structure and individual business procedures. Assess your communication and personality styles for compatibility.

Another promising possibility is when a financial investor or an aspiring entrepreneur and an experienced salon owner find a beneficial business arrangement.

Ask your friends about their experiences with business partnerships. You will hear horror stories about how one partner ran off with all the money and left the other in a mess. Others will tell you they were very successful and it was a joyful experience. Only you can determine if a partnership will benefit you and your dreams.

Tip: Choosing to have a partner is a very important decision, not to be taken lightly. A good partnership could make your entire life so much easier and more joyful. An incompatible partnership, just like a bad marriage, could leave you hurt, bitter, and resentful.

No BIG Mistakes: How to Choose a Partner

Exercise #1: Answer the following questions to get more insight on your decision to become a partner.

1. What are your reasons for wanting to share your business with another person?

2. Do you truly want a partnership or is it because of financial need?

3. Assess your character to determine if you have the temperament to involve another person in your business. Do you prefer to control all situations and make all decisions?

4. If you like things done in a certain way, you may have trouble with not having total control. Envision and then write down the qualities of the perfect potential partner:

Exercise #2:
Start interviewing candidates whom you would consider associating with on a daily basis. Exchange your dreams, goals, and concerns. Ask the same questions to the prospective partner that you would ask yourself when starting up a business. Below is a list of questions you and a potential partner will use to identify your business aspirations. Photocopy the page for your partner, then compare your answers:

1. What kind of salon image do you want to project?

2. What are your business strengths?

3. What are your business weaknesses?

4. If you are a previous business owner, what lessons did you learn from your last effort at entrepreneurship?

5. How could you improve upon your past performance?

6. What would be an appropriate location?

7. What work schedule would you choose?

8. What type of atmosphere would you desire? What color choices?

9. What type of client would you prefer?

10. What type of employee would you hire?

11. Are you comfortable with hiring decisions?

12. Are you comfortable with firing decisions?

13. Which products and services would you incorporate into your business?

14. What would be your role in this business operation?

15. How would financial and bookkeeping matters be executed?

16. What are your goals and expectations for this business?

17. List all the things that are important to you in shaping your business.

18. What would be the price range of your salon?

19. What style of salon exterior and signage would you choose?

20. Who would be responsible for making major purchases?

21. Who would pay the bills and make payroll?

22. Who would order supplies, stock, and price them?

23. Who would clean the salon or would you hire a cleaning service?

24. How much will you spend to market your salon?

25. What promotions or advertising will you use to market the salon?

26. Who will choose the name, logo, signs, phone book/internet listing, etc?

27. How often will you have staff meetings or educational training and who will preside?

28. How will you share the profits?

Become a Corporation

A corporation is an artificial entity with an unlimited life span empowered by the state to carry on a specific line of business. Shareholders own the corporation and are liable for damages only to the extent of their holdings.

The corporate advantages are limited liability, investment liquidity, unlimited life span and ability to raise capital. The corporation shields the personal assets, including real estate, of the shareholders. A shareholder is liable for the corporation's debt and other obligations only to the extent of his or her investment.

"The disadvantages are that the corporate business involves higher taxes and fees, stricter laws concerning business operations, and more elaborate bookkeeping."

A public disclosure is required. All of these disadvantages make it more expensive to maintain than a sole proprietorship or partnership.

You must obtain a charter from the state. Management is subject to taxation and regulation by the state. The board of directors are managers who determine policies and make decisions. Profits are divided according to the number of shares owned by each stockholder. A company officer will file the articles of incorporation with the Secretary of State and schedule maybe one annual corporate meeting. You can fill out the paperwork yourself or have an attorney do it for you. Attorneys charge anywhere from $500-1,000 or more for their services. You divide and issue stock certificates among company principals and investors. State law requires annual minutes from meetings and corporate documents to be in order.

A corporate structure is the best choice if you plan to

franchise your business or open a chain of salons.

You may go to a great deal of expense and trouble in setting up a corporation, then later find that such a complex form of business is unnecessary. If in doubt, always seek the advice of an attorney.

Making it BIG by Purchasing an Established Salon

Potential entrepreneurs have another BIG decision to make. Will they purchase an established salon or a franchise salon?

Many potential entrepreneurs feel more comfortable with purchasing an established salon, which has the following advantages:

1. The costly start-up expenditures have all been done for you i.e., plumbing, electrical, equipment, decor, and scouting a successful location etc.

2. You will get an established clientele and trained employees.

3. You'll be trained in existing salon procedures.

4. Accounting and tax rates have been established. Ask to see the profit and loss statement and approximate revenues. Be sure you understand what you are getting into, but keep in mind that many businesses have good and bad years. Hair salons are no exception. Ask your accountant to review the statements and give you advice.

5. The salon will be established with sales people and hopefully have good credit with suppliers. I would suggest checking with suppliers who have had business dealings with the prospective salon.

6. The salon is also established in the community. You may reap additional rewards if the previous owners' reputation is of good integrity.

Purchasing an established business has the following disadvantages:

1. Present employees may be set in their ways. They may have a difficult time adjusting to new rules and procedures. Some stylists may be opposed to switching to a discount or quick cut business when they are accustomed to a higher priced personal service salon, and vice versa. You may find yourself in the midst of a power struggle with employees or they may go elsewhere.

2. Does the salon have a poor reputation in the community? Changing it may take a lot of time, money and effort. Some business locations just never seem to do well no matter who takes over. We've all seen store fronts in which every new business stays for a short time, then either moves out or fails. It's best to investigate reasons why a location in which you are interested never appears to support a business.

3. If you make a distinct change in business procedures right away, you might risk losing valued employees. The key here is to teach employees to expect, welcome and enjoy change. Of course, there is always the possibility that employees will welcome changes from the tired old format.

4. Re-education is difficult. Many stylists will resist the re-education process if you introduce all new lines of product. Seasoned stylists often remain loyal to products with a proven performance.

Hair color formulas and permanent wave procedures are

often difficult to duplicate with an unfamiliar product line. Mistakes discredit the stylist, and jeopardize the client/employee relationship.

Sometimes clients rebel if you switch products because they too have developed product loyalty. They've been trained how to use particular products and may be unwilling to take a chance on an unproven product. Clients are especially concerned that hair colors will not be comparable.

5. Major adjustments could become costly if you need to upgrade equipment, change the floor plan, or increase your space.

Where and How to Purchase a Salon

Options for purchasing a salon:

1. Call several commercial real estate agents to find which salons are for sale.

2. Ask your family, friends and acquaintances if they know about a salon for sale.

3. Look in the advertisement section of your newspaper or on the internet for salons.

4. Many beauty supply houses have a bulletin board where salons are listed.

5. Craig's List has commercial salon listings.

If you know the area where you want to purchase a salon, you may consider asking salon owners in that area if they are willing to sell. I've been told that everything is for sale for the right price. If you find an owner willing to accommodate you, then the process begins.

Ask to audit the books, and interview employees and clients. You must determine if the *asking price* is fair to both you and the seller. Ask your attorney to establish a fair selling price. This will depend upon the location, the cost and condition of furnishings, the cooperation of employees, and the loyalty of the salons' clientele. You must also negotiate a new contract with the landlord.

Tip: The process is much simpler when you let a commercial real estate agent act as an intermediary and handle your affairs. You'll be paying them a commission to take care of the details for you and the owner.

How to Pay for an Existing Salon

Secret: If you decide to buy an existing salon, it should virtually pay for itself. Buy your salon on contract from the owner. Establish a fair price, make the down payment and pay the balance and interest charges over a reasonable period of time, ideally three years. Make sure your payments are low enough so you have enough cash flow to pay your salon bills and still make a profit.

Risk Assessment

As in all new business ventures, you must assess the possibility that something will go wrong. There is an element of risk with every business. Include the effects of competition on your business, a recession, unfavorable industry trends, potential illness or injury, loss of key personnel, or anything that may prevent you from carrying on your business in the most efficient way. Develop a plan for troubleshooting the most significant risks.

Eight Ways to Finance Your New Salon

There are many ways in which to finance your new salon:

1. Use your personal savings.

2. Get a loan from relatives or friends.

3. Get a credit line from your bank.

4. Contact the Small Business Administration or an Entrepreneurship Program for classes and a guaranteed bank loan.

5. Buy on contract from the owner.

6. Tap into your stocks or bonds.

7. Find a partner who has capital.

8. Seek a home equity loan or a second mortgage.

These are just some of the ideas you might want to consider when starting your own salon business. Partnerships and home equity loans are risky options. You will need an attorney to draw up a contract if you decide on a partnership. Get a home equity loan only if you are absolutely sure of your business success, otherwise you may end up losing you home if you can't pay back the loan.

A friend or relative may be a good source for a loan. Be sure to treat them with the same consideration that you would give to a formal lending institution. Make an official presentation and submit a loan proposal and a business plan. Clearly delineate the terms of the loan and the repayment schedule. It can be a good experience if you do it correctly and set boundaries. My advice is to investigate all possibilities and use common sense.

Make it BIG with a Franchise

Franchises like Supercuts, Fantastic Sams, Great Clips, Inc., Cost Cutters, Regis, Magicuts and ProCuts Hair Salons have become increasingly popular and successful.

The purpose of buying a franchise is to take advantage of the franchisers proven expertise and well-known name, as well as national advertising. For a varying fee, they will help train you in the technical and financial phases of the business. Most franchisers will offer assistance on all or part of the following:

1. Counseling
2. Help with site selection
3. Lease negotiations
4. Operating manuals
5. Video tape training
6. Product knowledge
7. Scheduling appointments
8. Marketing
9. Public relations
10. Staff hiring and motivation
11. Construction assistance
12. Insurance
13. Payroll
14. Continued support

Tip: Sometimes the franchiser will offer partial financing to qualified buyers.

Some of the disadvantages of buying a franchise:

The franchiser might present an unrealistic account of the working capital required. Many franchise buyers try to qualify without being honest about their own finances. An undercapitalized business is very soon in trouble. Another disadvantage is that you must do business their way. Your costs are the basic fee and quite possibly a monthly fee. You will also pay for the equipment package, plumbing, electrical, decor, supplies and more. My research suggests that costs are a minimum of $30,000 – $100,000 cash investment and a minimum of $250,000 net worth. Look at www.HairFranchiseExperts.com for their information.

There are many franchise operations from which to choose, so investigate each one thoroughly before you buy. Check on prospective companies through the Better Business Bureau and trade organizations. Request names and telephone numbers of franchise owners to get first hand information. You may also request a financial statement of the franchiser to determine the stability of the company.

In Conclusion

This chapter guided you in making that critical first decision about business form. Review all the advantages and disadvantages and choose the business identity that feels right to you and make the most sense.

Notes:

CHAPTER FIVE
Identify Your Competition

Knowing who your competition is may be the single most important piece of information in your arsenal of success tools. Research the community in which you plan to open your new salon. Study all the salons in that area and pay attention to what they are doing or *not doing*.

Tip: Never underestimate a minor competitor. They have goals too, and sometimes arise to beat out the competition. In the small town where I lived was a little beauty shop that didn't appear to have much activity. All of a sudden, the owner started opening discount haircutting businesses all over the area. Her business was a booming success.

Use the following list of questions to get the scoop on who they are and how they do business. This information will let you know what products and services are not being offered and how you fit in. The difference you make could be the key to your success.

You'll use this information again when you develop your marketing campaign, so don't skip over this important research. It may hold the key to your success.

Know Who You're Up Against: Eleven Critical Questions

1. List just five of your major and minor competitors.

    A.
    B.
    C.
    D.
    E.

2. What is the image and atmosphere of these businesses? Are any similar to the image you have in mind?

    A.
    B.
    C.
    D.
    E.

3. What is the size of your competing salons? How many employees do they have?

    A.
    B.
    C.
    D.
    E.

4. What services and brand name products do they offer?

    A.
    B.
    C.
    D.

E.

5. What is their fee structure?
   A.
   B.
   C.
   D.
   E.

6. What unique characteristics set them apart from the masses?
   A.
   B.
   C.
   D.
   E.

7. What type of client does this salon attract?
   A.
   B.
   C.
   D.
   E.

8. Describe your competition's marketing strategies:
   A.
   B.
   C.
   D.
   E.

9. What are their strengths?
   A.
   B.

C.
D.
E.

10. What are their weaknesses?
    A.
    B.
    C.
    D.
    E.

11. How close in proximity are they to your potential location?

    A.
    B.
    C.
    D.
    E.

More information about your competition is included in *Chapter 18: How to Market Your Salon for BIG Profits.* You'll also use this information in the next chapter when you write your business plan.

Tip: Be aware that too many salons in your area will inhibit growth and profits. Find a need that isn't being met and your business could *outshine* all the rest.

One of the most foolish things I ever did for a client was to help her navigate her way around the salon business. She told me she was a hairdresser at one point in her life, and I didn't think she was serious about getting back into it. She asked me to assess a salon for sale in our small town. I reluctantly went with her and we established it as a bad deal. I figured she would give it up, but she eventually found a place on her own. Some months later she not only opened her own salon in our community, but took one of my busiest employees with her.

It became a financially challenging circumstance for me, at least for a while. The employee she took with her was problematic, so in a way she did me a big favor. I never did hear much about her business until it closed up less than a year later. Many people think owning a business is easy. It's not … but some entrepreneurs make it look easy because they have such a passion for serving others. If you have that passion, you'll leave your competition in the dust!

In Conclusion

If it appears that I'm beleaguering this point, it's because it's so important to get a handle on your competition. Know what they are doing and do it better. Otherwise you are just another small fish in a big pond rather than a BIG fish in a small pond.

Notes:

CHAPTER SIX
How to Develop
a Winning Business Plan

Your business plan is the blueprint for your success. When architects design a new building they provide a blueprint to outline a strong and durable foundation as well as its supporting structures. During the development phases of your salon, you will find it valuable to create a blueprint that outlines your ideas and research.

Your objective at this point is to launch a new business or expand a small promising one. Whether you're a potential salon owner or a seasoned entrepreneur, you will find value in being organized and knowing how your venture will operate.

The process of creating a business plan forces you to take a realistic, objective, and critical look at your business in its entirety. Whether you are just beginning or have been in business for several years, it's never too late to develop clarity. You don't have to be an expert to develop an effective plan but to be efficient the plan is necessary.

You'll have an opportunity at the end of this chapter to create your own business plan.

The Three Functions of a Business Plan

1. It can be used to develop ideas about how the business should be conducted.

2. It is a helpful tool against which a businessperson can assess their actual performance over time.

3. It could help raise money to run the business.

The business plan is the chief instrument for communicating your ideas to potential partners and associates, bankers and employees. It allows you to give clarity to any vague thoughts you may have.

A business plan is a written summary of what you plan to accomplish and how you intend to organize your resources to attain those goals. You will ask yourself these important questions:

1. What are you offering?
2. Who are your clients?
3. What needs are your services satisfying?
4. How will your potential clients find you?
5. How much money do you plan on making?
6. What actions do you plan to take that will ensure success?
7. How will you keep focused and motivated?

Tip: As business owners, we get caught up in daily activities and forget to take care of business. This can cause us to miss out on opportunities.

It's important to become aware of what your finances really are, and how far they can be stretched if possible. It's fine to dream of great things, and you must also be realistic. A business plan may assist you in discovering something previously overlooked. It's best use is to identify your strengths and weaknesses.

A Tool for Bankers and Venture Capitalists

Venture capitalists, banks or anyone who plans to lend you money will need to see certain elements in your business plan. They want to know the name of your salon, and what legal form you have chosen. If you are a corporation, you'll add the date and State where your business is incorporated. List the founders' names. Describe the nature of your business. Is it a hair salon, hair and nails, a spa, or a barber shop? Do you own any trademarks? What is your geographical area? You will need to furnish a physical description of the salon. They will want to know your major suppliers and a list of major customers.

Explain the factors that set you apart from other businesses in your category. Your market must be well-defined, detailing both existing and potential customers. If you are quitting a salon to open your own, list the clients who will most likely follow you. Remember to ask them for references. Include your target market research for the area where you will relocate.

Tip: Here's the key - know who your customers are, how much they spend, what products they buy and which services they require? Those financial numbers will work in your favor.

Set firm target dates for business operations:

1. Establish where and why you've chosen a location and when you intend to lease the space.

2. Determine where and when you will purchase salon equipment and supplies. How much will you spend?

3. Note the date of your opening, and any promotions you intend to implement.

4. Include the number of employees you intend to hire or already

have working for you. Describe any employee benefits that you intend to provide.

Back up everything with solid financial projections. You must forecast your cash flow and state the application of funds for the next three years. State your annual sales last year, and your profit or loss. State the type of business loan you are seeking. Add what types of insurance coverage you plan to purchase. They must know if your real estate is leased or owned. Explain your bank relationships and your credit lines.

Include a list of competitors from *Chapter Five: Identify Your Competition*. Describe the economic state of the industry and specify what percentage of the market share you now have and what percentage you hope to capture. Also focus on how you will implement your pricing concepts and promotional strategies.

"Your basic plan should highlight marketing, operations, financial projections and management."

It's a good idea to furnish copies of business cards, brochures, mailers, publicity releases, newspaper and magazine articles etc. List your web site if you have one. Describe your reputation and your experience. Determine what qualities set you apart from others who are in the same business. Include a projection of growth from your market research. Include the amount of Facebook Fans you have or how many Twitter followers. Submit a *typed* business plan (Show business savvy).

When developing a business plan remember that nothing is written in stone, and your plans may need to be revised as necessary. A financier will assess your plans and base the decision to give you a loan upon this information.

Writing a Business Plan is Like Writing a Resume

Writing a business plan is much like writing a resume, except it's a bit more detailed. You must shape and tailor the inside information to suit the needs of the lender (Loan officer, venture capitalist, friend). Don't make it so long and complex that the reader will become bored with it. Make it comprehensive, because the reader probably won't spend more than a short time reading it. A business plan can help you avoid a business venture that is doomed to failure.

If you don't feel confident to write your own business plan, you may want to seek the advice of a professional.

The main idea is to show precisely how the money is going to be used. This important information will give backers an idea of what you are all about, and if you are physically, mentally, and emotionally capable of starting and operating a business.

Tip: No matter how well written and documented, the plan must be followed in order to succeed. All the best intentions in the world are meaningless if you don't follow through with the plan.

Business Plan Components

1. Executive Summary: The executive summary should be less than two pages. Most people write this last, as a powerful summary of the business they want to provide. The SBA describes the executive summary in this way:

"The executive summary is Part 1 of the business plan and is the most important section of your plan. It provides a concise overview of the entire plan, along with a history of your company. This section tells your reader where your company is and where you want to take it. It's the first thing your readers see; therefore, it is the thing that will either grab their interest and make them want to keep reading or make them want to put it down and forget about it. More than anything else, this section is important because it tells the reader why you think your business idea will be successful." – Resource – web site: http://www.sba.gov/content/business-plan-executive-summary

Tip: Focus on your skills, your experience, your background and the decisions that led you to start this business.

2. Business Description and Vision:

Include your mission statement, company vision, a history of the company, and a list of all the principals of your company. What is your business's expected growth and potential?

A. **Determine long-range goals:** Use your goals from Chapter Three. Plan a financial forecast and show how you will achieve your long-term goals.

B. **Determine short-term goals**: Use your short term goals from Chapter Three.

C. **Management Team:** Explain your business's management structure and the abilities that will make your efforts successful. Include your management team's experience, areas of specialization, and interaction within the industry as well as within the community. List personnel, expected turnover rate, any benefit program or incentives. Add resumes of key personnel, business and personal references, reputation, capabilities, and attitude. List salaries or commissions, and enclose proposed contracts with employees.

If you are a sole proprietor, you may not have a management team. Or you can include your advisory team: lawyer, accountant, marketing consultant etc. List any management or supervisory experience you may have from a former career or position. Talk about a management course you took. Do you have a friend or relative who can coach you? Lenders are looking for business owners who are credible and competent.

3. Definition of the Market: What is the history, size, trend of product or service, suppliers and references, and size of clientele? What are the best seasonal times?

Describe any potential changes in the neighborhood that may contribute to your success. Is there a factory, college or apartment complex going into your neighborhood? List any properties that you own. Explain the state of your equipment; it's condition, value estimate, owned or leased etc.

   A. Marketing plan, analysis, and strategy: List your strategy for advertising, publicity and promotion, competition location, sales earnings, percentage of market, new competition, and comparative prices. How will you reach your target market? What the demand is for your services and products? What promotions, advertisements or publicity will get you noticed in a BIG way? What distribution supplier will you use: internet, newspaper, radio, direct mail etc.? Review the marketing chapter for more information about marketing your salon.

   B. Identify your target market: Read through the marketing chapter in this book for tips on how to create a strategy and reach your target market.

4. Description of Products and Services: List all the services on your salon menu and a list of products you'll be using and selling. Explain how your services and products are competitive and the advantages you have over your competition. Include a brochure and how much your services and products sell for.

5. Operational Plan, Timetables and Strategy: You'll list your start-up costs and profit and loss statements. What are the financial projections for your business? Forms are shown in this chapter.

6. Ownership and Equity: Include anything substantial that you might own: Commercial real estate or a home.

7. Potential Pitfalls: You may or may not want to include this in your business plan. It is good to be aware of any potential pitfalls. They can prevent you from making critical errors. Instead it might be better to wait a year or two for economic conditions to improve.

List any concerns you foresee. Are there many unemployed individuals who are not finding work and therefore not spending money? Will the colleges and Universities be out of session when you open? Note anything that might deter your business from taking off in the first year or two.

Follow these forms to complete your business plan. You can also find business plan templates at your local office supply store, on the internet or from the Small Business Administration.

Business name: _____

Business address: _____

Business phone: _____

Owners name: _____

Owners home address: _____

Owners home phone: _____

Brief Business Description:
How long the business has been established? List the services offered and summarize your business experience and philosophy:

Statement of Current Business Financial Status:

Purpose, Priorities and Goals

A. Overall Career Goals:
State your purpose, vision, mission statement and at least six priorities for your career:

B. Long Range Goals:
State your long range (3-5 year) purpose, at least six priorities and at least two goals per priority for your career:

C. Short Term Goals:
List your short term (1-2 years) purpose, at least six priorities and at least three goals per priority for your career:

Definition of the Business

A. Describe your location: _____

B. Define in detail the major services offered and prices:

C. List other services offered and prices: _____

D. List special products used and prices: _____

E. List all equipment and prices: _____

F. Unique features:
Describe the unique features that distinguish your business from others: include attributes such as experience, variety of services/ techniques, pricing, location, product sales, equipment, supplies, management abilities and capital.

G. Product sales:
Define your position in the chain of distribution, list the types of suppliers that you buy from and specify the types of clients that purchase products.

Client Profile

This is a descriptive analysis of your current and potential clients: who are they, what are their interests, and where can you find them? Include each of your target markets.

1. Target Market No. 1

2. Target Market No. 2

3. Target Market No. 3

Income Potential

* Seek data from reliable sources

1. Describe the existing business conditions. Where do you stand in the current state of the art? Can you get this information from trade magazines?

2. Describe the projections and trends for your profession:

Locally _____

Nationally _____

3. List the average income for salons in your category:
The first six months   _____
The first year   _____
The second year   _____
The third year   _____

4. List the average number of clients per stylist:
The first six months   _____
The first year   _____
The second year   _____
The third year   _____

Marketing

This section is about creating strategies to inform potential customers of your business: getting your share of the market.

1. List the benefits of your services and products:

2. What are the distinguishing characteristics of your products and services?

3. How will your potential clients recognize the difference?

4. What is your position statement?

5. List the amenities to be absorbed in pricing: educational materials, samples, supplies, coffee, tea and food, etc.

6. Describe your competitions' effect on pricing:

Maintenance and Safety

1. What are your security needs? How will you handle clients who are under the influence of alcohol or drugs? How will you handle clients who steal products or other clients' belongings?

2. List your procedures for repairs, maintenance, and cleaning:

Analysis of Your Competition

Look in the yellow pages, the internet, or Facebook fan pages. Interview clients, or request brochures to discover more information. Call competitive salons and ask their prices. Send a friend to get a price list and see how many clients are there on a busy or slow day. Ask the friend to notice competitor's image and size of service areas.

1. Number of salons in town, city, or area: (within a two or three mile radius)

2. Number of salons specializing in your area of expertise:

3. Names of your closest competitors. Include the types of services offered, their strengths and weaknesses:

4. Weaknesses your business has in comparison to your competition:

5. Steps you'll take to overcome those weaknesses:

Competition's Marketing Assessment

The first phase in planning your promotional campaign is appraising the competition. List major competitors and describe their marketing strategies. Use the information from the previous chapter.

1. Major competitor #1

2. Major competitor #2

3. Major competitor #3

4. Major competitor #4

5. Major competitor #5

Promotion and Advertising Plan

1. Marketing your services:

Media	Goals	Timeline	Budget
____	____	____	____
____	____	____	____
____	____	____	____

2. Description and product cost:
   A. Inside displays, posters and signs:

   B. Outside displays: window, billboards, sandwich
   board, signs:

3. Promotional budget per year:
   A. Total cost of media $_____
   B. Total cost for product promotion $_____
   C. Total promotional budget $_____

Outline Your Marketing Plan

Goal   Target Date
1. _____   _____
2. _____   _____
3. _____   _____

1. How will your marketing strategies enable you to succeed?

2. What are some of the areas that require special attention?

Additional Guidelines

Is your business plan for your own personal use? If so, you can make it as thorough as necessary. If you are presenting the plan to a financial lending institution, then you will need to find out their requirements. Below is a list of items they may require.

- Personal net worth statement
- Copies of last two year's income statements and balance sheets
- List of client commitments
- Copies of business legal agreements
- Credit status reports
- News articles about you or your business
- Copies of promotional material
- Letters of recommendation from your clients
- Personal references

Financial Forecast

1. **Calculate your break-even analysis:** This is the point where total costs equal total income. This will need to be updated periodically to accurately reflect your business's growth.

2. **Describe the loan requirements:** The amount needed, the terms and the date by which it's required.

3. **State the purpose of the loan:** Detail the areas of your business to be financed.

4. Provide a statement of the owner's equity.

5. **List any outstanding loans:** Include balance due, repayment terms, purpose of the loan and status.

6. State your current operating line of credit, the amount and security held.

-FINANCIAL FORECAST-

Opening Balance Sheet
Date: _____

-ASSETS-

Current Assets

Cash and bank accounts $_____

Accounts receivable $_____

Inventory $_____

Other current assets $_____

TOTAL CURRENT ASSETS (A) $_____
Fixed Assets

Property owned $_____

Furniture and equipment $_____

Business automobile $_____

Leasehold improvements $_____

Other fixed assets $_____

TOTAL FIXED ASSETS   (B) $_____
TOTAL ASSETS (A + B =X) $_____

-LIABILITIES-

Current Liabilities (due within next 12 months)
Bank loans $_____

Other loans $_____

Accounts payable $_____

Other current liabilities $_____

TOTAL CURRENT LIABILITIES (C) $_____

Mortgages $_____

Long-term loans $_____

Other long-term liabilities $_____

TOTAL LONG-TERM LIABILITIES (D) $_____
TOTAL LIABILITIES $_____

NET WORTH $_____

TOTAL NET WORTH AND LIABILITIES $_____

Business Income and Expense Forecast
for the Next 12 Months-

One year estimate ending _____, Date: _____

-PROJECTED NUMBER OF CLIENTS-

For your services   _____
For your products   _____

TOTAL NUMBER OF CLIENTS

-PROJECTED INCOME-

Appointments $_____
Product Sales $_____
Other $_____

TOTAL INCOME (A) $_____

-PROJECTED EXPENSES-

Start-up costs $_____

Monthly expenses (x 12) $_____
Annual expenses $_____
TOTAL EXPENSE (B) $_____

TOTAL OPERATING PROFIT (OR LOSS (A-B)$_____

CAPITAL REQUIRED FOR THE NEXT 12 MONTHS
                                                  $_____

In Conclusion

You business plan should tell a compelling story about your business. It needs to explain who, what, when, where, and why. Make it focused and clear. Define specific business objectives and goals. Remember to update it regularly.

Notes:

CHAPTER SEVEN
Your Legal Responsibilities

State and Federal taxes and licenses are legal responsibilities with which you must comply.

Your State Board License

You will need a salon license from your State Board of Cosmetology. You will have to pay a license fee, show a manager's license and pass an inspection before you receive a salon license. Check with the state board of beauty culturist examiners in your state for current laws and requirements.

State Board Inspections

Inspectors from your State Board of Cosmetology make unannounced inspections of all licensed hair salons. They basically check for overall cleanliness of salon and personnel, displayed licenses, use of wet and dry sanitizers, covered waste receptacles and other sanitation requirements.

In some states, the salon owner is financially penalized for not displaying the state license and Health and Safety Rules, not using sanitizers (disinfectants and fungicidals), or keeping poor sanitary conditions. Check with your State Board of Cosmetology about their rules and regulations.

Tax Deductions, Knowing the Law

It is beyond the scope of this book to offer tax law, so it is in your best interests to speak with an accountant or tax advisor. If you are self-employed and earn more than $600.00 a year, you must file:

• Schedule SE: Social Security Self-Employment Tax Form.
• Schedule C: Sole Proprietorship Business or Profession Profit or Loss Form.
• Form 1040: U.S. Individual Income Tax Return.
• Form 1040 ES: Estimated tax for Individuals (If you expect to owe taxes).
• Form 1099: Any employer who pays more than $600.00 to a self-employed person must report that payment to the IRS and to the subcontractor.
• Form 1065-K1: Partnership Information Return (for a business owned by two or more individuals).

Many legal deductions are allowed if you are engaged in a trade or business. I will list some of the deductions, but get more detailed information from your accountant. Remember that laws change yearly.

Tip: Remember to keep all receipts, canceled checks and expense account records where required.

A tentative list of deductions:
1. Accounting expense
2. Advertising expenses
3. Alteration of business property
4. Attorney and accountant fees

5. Automobile expenses
6. Gifts to employees (there are dollar limits)
7. Conference expenses
8. Wages
9. Depreciation of equipment
10. Discounts allowed to customers
11. Dues to clubs and trade associations etc.
12. Safety deposit box for storage of business property or papers
13. Freight charges
14. Utilities
15. Building expenses and improvements
16. Insurance premiums
17. Interest on loans for business purposes
18. Losses, if connected to business: burglary, building damage, business ventures, abandoned equipment and theft if not covered by insurance.
19. Maintenance of business property
20. Moving costs
21. Newspapers and magazines
22. Towel service
23. Passport fees
24. Postage
25. Rent
26. Social Security taxes paid by employer
27. Payment-workmen's compensation

Business Use of Home

The laws pertaining to business use of the home change yearly. You may be able to deduct a home-office expense if you have a room devoted entirely to office space. Your telephone bill may be partially deductible and any other expenses generally associated with office expenditures. Confer with an accountant to determine whether the owner of a hair salon may deduct home office expenditures.

Travel and Entertainment

Keep accurate records in order to substantiate all travel and entertainment expenses. In regards to clients' gifts, you are allowed to declare a certain dollar amount per year. The deduction for business-related meals and entertainment is limited. Check with your accountant, as dollar amounts change from year to year. If you travel any distance for business, the actual transportation and lodging costs are usually deductible. An unusual number of trips to exotic locales might be ground for an audit.

The records you keep must be supported by adequate evidence such as receipts, canceled checks, and credit card statements. Keep a journal with all pertinent information: dates, time, place, business purpose, and names of persons entertained.

The customary and necessary expenses incurred on operating and maintaining a vehicle for business purposes is deductible according to the actual percentage of business use. The two methods for computing allowable expenses are the actual expenses at the business-use percentage or the total business mileage. The best evidence to support a transportation deduction is a logbook that shows the date, business purpose, destination, and mileage of all business travel.

Laws are constantly changing, so it is always in your best interests to ask questions of an accounting professional.

Business Mileage Record

Always keep a business mileage charge to prove your mileage in case you are audited. I suggest keeping a small notebook in your auto or making a spreadsheet for your records.

Build a table in Excel with 6 columns and as many rows as you need. Include these titles in your columns: date, destination, purpose, starting mileage, ending mileage, total mileage, and gas costs.

Date	Beginning Mileage	Ending Mileage	Purpose	Destination	Gas

File Your Tax Forms

These are the *approximate* dates for filing any required forms:

Jan. 15: Fourth installment of your previous years estimated tax

Jan. 31: Businesses must furnish 1099s to subcontractors

Employers must furnish W-2 statements to employees

Employers must file previous year's tax returns and pay taxes due.

Feb. 28: Businesses must file information returns with IRS (1099) Employers must send W-2 copies to Social Security Administration.

Mar. 15: Previous calendar year corporation income tax returns due.

April 15: Deadline for individual tax returns. In addition to Form 1040 (and appropriate accompanying schedule) include the requisite business forms such as: 1065 K-1, Schedules SE and C.

First installment of current years estimated tax.

July 15: Second installment of current years estimated tax.

Oct. 15: Third installment of current years estimated tax.

Generally, you must pay estimated tax if you expect to owe (after subtracting your withholding and credits) at least $500.00 in tax for this current year, and you expect your withholding and credits to be less than:

1. Ninety percent of the tax to be shown on current year tax return -or-

2. One hundred percent of the tax shown on the previous year tax return (given the return covered all twelve months).

The exception to this is if your previous year tax return showed a refund or the balance due was less than $500.00. Check the current amount.

IRS regulations require taxpayers to keep records and receipts for as long as they may be applicable to the enforcement of tax law. For income and expenses, this is usually the later of three years from the date the return was filed and for two years after the tax was paid. As always ask your accountant to update you on these laws. Records related to the purchase of real estate and equipment should be kept indefinitely. Copies of tax returns should be kept for ten years.

* Speak with a tax attorney as this information may or may not apply to you.

Regulations, Business Laws and Insurance Regulations

All businesses must comply with local and Federal laws regarding business activities. It is beyond the scope of this book to supply all the answers. I encourage you to seek the services of a professional accountant.

Under Federal law you will have to pay Social Security taxes, unemployment compensation and Federal Taxes.

If you have employees, you will need an employer identification number. To get an EIN, file form SS-4 with your local IRS office.

State law requires payment for workman's compensation and state sales tax (If you sell retail products and collect sales tax).

Your State Department of Revenue can answer your questions. Your accountant may also offer assistance.

Local regulations cover building and renovations.

Tip: Become aware of what the zoning laws are in your town or city. Contact your local zoning commission for information before you sign a lease. The Chamber of Commerce will also have information concerning regulations.

Insurance as a Safety Net

Insurance is a system of protection whereas you and an agent agree to terms of compensation whenever there is a business loss, fire or accident. Proper insurance is imperative for any small business. Your insurance needs will be different from many other businesses. Be sure to discuss your concerns with a qualified insurance agent. Shop around and get more than one bid for your insurance needs.

Small business insurance provides umbrella coverage for business losses in terms of general liability, business interruption, and product liability.

Your insurance requirements are for:

• **Malpractice:** This insurance refers to any damages or injuries a client might sustain from a product or service not performed properly. This basically means unintentional loss of hair and injury to the skin due to negligence or failure to perform at a professional skill level.

• **Premises liability:** Insurance to cover your rental space or unit.

• **Fire & theft:** Fire and theft covers equipment, furniture, supplies and documents.

• **Public liability:** This insurance covers the cost of injuries that occur on your property to business related visitors.

• **Business interruption insurance:** Personal disability insurance safeguards you from loss of income if you are unable to work due to illness or injury. You are paid a certain monthly amount if you are permanently disabled or a portion if you are partially disabled.

• **Partnership Insurance:** This insurance protects you against lawsuits arising from the actions or omissions by any of your business partners.

• **Medical Health Insurance:** Health insurance is used to help cover medical bills, particularly for complicated illnesses, injuries, and hospitalization.

• **Worker's Compensation:** If you have employees this insurance is required by law. It covers all of the costs that you as an employer would be required to pay for any injuries to an employee.

Tip: If your salon business is located in a shopping center, the lease will generally dictate how much liability insurance you are required to purchase, usually one million dollars. When shopping for insurance, get estimates from at least two reliable companies.

In Conclusion
It's best to know your legal responsibilities in advance. These legalities are common to most businesses and protect you, your employees, your clients and your business from penalties and/ or lawsuits.

CHAPTER EIGHT
Bookkeeping Made Easy

Bookkeeping is an important part of monitoring your business. Accurate records will allow you to instantly have an overview of your salon's financial picture. At a glance, you should be able to see if you are making a profit or losing your shirt.

First of all, I recommend that you seek the services of a professional accountant to help set up your books, especially if you don't have good accounting skills. If you are computer literate, you could purchase an accounting software package from software vendors. Intuit QuickBooks® is a good computerized accounting package.

The most critical time to talk to an accountant is at tax time. Tax returns are complex, even for a small business. Laws are constantly changing, so getting the right advice will keep you on the legal side and away from receiving penalties.

Tip: It is generally recommended that you pay your supply bills when they are due, unless you receive a discount for early payment.

Suggestions for accurate bookkeeping:
1. Keep your business checking account separate from your

personal one. It's easier to check your account and select deductions at tax time.

2. Keep records of receipts, bank statements, copies of tax returns and ledger sheets for seven years to protect yourself against an audit.

3. Keep lists of inventory, equipment, furniture and client files.

4. Keep mileage logs if you use your car for business, and a list of all incidentals. It doesn't need to be complicated, but it does need to be done.

Opening Your First Business Bank Account

One of the first things you must do as a business owner is to set up a business checking account. You will be required to register your business with a federal office. This is called a d.b.a. and it means 'doing business as.' Many banks will not allow you to open a business checking without a d.b.a.

Find a bank located near your business. You will need to go there regularly for change, nightly deposits and monthly/ quarterly tax deposits. Your employees will probably cash their paychecks there too.

When you open your business checking account, make sure you choose the type of checkbook with two receipts, one for your records and one for the employees' records (If you have employees). There are many ways to organize your check data. Include your (d.b.a.) business name, your personal name and position, address, phone number, and your web site. Your position may be founder, proprietor, owner or whatever appeals to you. This last bit of information gives you credibility if you use your checks for purchasing items from department stores, or any business that does not personally know you.

To avoid confusion, it is beneficial to keep all of your accounts: business checking, personal checking, savings, mortgage, annuity, safety deposit box, IRA, etc., with the same bank. This procedure also establishes a good relationship with the bank in case you need to ask for a loan for future expansion or other needs.

Exercise:
Make a list of all the details you want on the front of your check. Write some samples of how you want your business checks to look. What bank will you use?

Managing Payroll

One of your most pressing business activities is to manage payroll. Yes, your employees will expect a check for services performed. Make payroll for your employees either weekly or biweekly. Your payroll responsibilities are required by government agencies: federal, state or local. There will be withholding amounts from your employees' compensation to cover income tax, social security, Medicare, and other payments. These are called trust fund taxes because the money is held in a special trust fund for the U.S. government.

Late or inaccurate deposits may result in penalties or interest charges. Ask you accountant to help you get the information you need to withhold payroll taxes or you can use your computer software program.

Use these steps for managing payroll:

1. Get your Federal Employer Identification Number (FEIN). This is the number that the U.S. government uses to identify your business. You'll use this number on all your payroll and tax documents.

2. Get a state I.D. number too.

3. Each of your employees needs to fill out a W-4 form. This form will show how many allowances are claimed for withholding tax purposes.

4. You can either do it yourself or hire a payroll service. My accountant guided me through the process and I did payroll myself each week. It's not that complicated but does take a little time. You can also do payroll in Quickbooks or other accounting software.

Start-up Costs Worksheet

<u>Item</u>   <u>Estimated Expense</u>

Item	Estimated Expense
Open checking account	$_____
Telephone installation	$_____
Equipment	$_____
First & last month's rent, security deposit, others.	$_____
Supplies	$_____
Business cards, stationary, brochures, etc.	$_____
Advertising and promotion package	$_____
Decorating and remodeling	$_____
Furniture and fixtures	$_____
Legal and professional fees	$_____
Insurance	$_____

Utility deposits $_____
Beginning inventory $_____
Installation of fixtures and equipment $_____
Licenses and permits $_____
Other $_____
TOTAL $_____

Fixed Annual Expense Worksheet

<u>Item</u>	<u>Estimated Expense</u>
Property insurance	$_____
Business auto insurance	$_____
Licenses and permits	$_____
Liability insurance	$_____
Disability insurance	$_____
Professional industry membership	$_____
Fees (legal, accounting, etc.)	$_____
Taxes	$_____
Other	$_____
TOTAL	$_____

Monthly Business Expense

Expense	Estimated Monthly Cost	X12
Rent	$_____	$_____
Utilities	$_____	$_____
Telephone	$_____	$_____
Bank fees	$_____	$_____
Supplies	$_____	$_____
Stationary/biz cards	$_____	$_____
Education (seminars/books/tapes/etc.)	$_____	$_____
Biz auto (payments/gas/repairs/etc.)	$_____	$_____

Advertising/promotion $_____ $_____
Postage $_____ $_____
Entertainment $_____ $_____
Repair/cleaning/maintenance $_____ $_____
Travel $_____ $_____
Business loan payments $_____ $_____
Salary $_____ $_____
Staff salaries/commissions $_____ $_____

Misc. insurance $_____ $_____
Taxes $_____ $_____
Professional fees $_____ $_____
Decorations $_____ $_____
Equipment/fixtures $_____ $_____
Furniture $_____ $_____
Inventory $_____ $_____
Other $_____ $_____

TOTAL MONTHLY $_____
TOTAL YEARLY $_____

Cash Flow Forecast

Below is a chart for your cash flow forecast. Make 12 copies and fill out one for each month.

	Month	
	Estimated	**Actual**
Beginning Cash	$_____	$_____
Plus Monthly Fees From:		
Fees	$_____	$_____
Sales	$_____	$_____

Loans	$_____	$_____
Other	$_____	$_____

Total Cash & Income $_____ $_____

Expenses:

Rent	$_____	$_____
Utilities	$_____	$_____
Telephone	$_____	$_____
Bank fees	$_____	$_____
Supplies	$_____	$_____
Stationary/business cards	$_____	$_____
Insurance	$_____	$_____
Dues	$_____	$_____
Education	$_____	$_____
Auto	$_____	$_____
Advertising/promotion	$_____	$_____
Postage	$_____	$_____
Entertainment	$_____	$_____
Repair & maintenance	$_____	$_____
Travel	$_____	$_____
Business loan payments	$_____	$_____
Licenses & permits	$_____	$_____
Salary	$_____	$_____
Staff salaries	$_____	$_____
Staff commissions	$_____	$_____
Taxes	$_____	$_____
Professional fees	$_____	$_____
Interior decorations	$_____	$_____
Furniture & fixtures	$_____	$_____
Equipment	$_____	$_____
Inventory	$_____	$_____
Other expenses	$_____	$_____
TOTAL EXPENSES	$_____	$_____
ENDING CASH	$_____	$_____

Accounting and Control

1. Who does the bookkeeping? (You or an accountant?)_____
2. Management reports - frequency
   - A. Balance sheets _____
   - B. Condition of client accts. _____
   - C. Profit and loss statements_____
   - D. Expense reports _____
   - E. Forecasting _____
   - F. Service reports _____
   - G. Sales reports _____
   - H. Inventory reports _____

Break-even analysis - determine your fixed and variable costs, estimate your monthly rent, utilities, insurance, wages, cost of supplies and products. Find total costs. Determine sales volume from services and products.

In salon business: subtract commissions on services and products first, then salaries. Subtract overhead from the balance to determine break even point and realize rest as profit.

Raising Your Prices

Determine profit potential by the effects of raising either product or service prices. Project for the future, and revise your prices as rent and other overhead variables increase or decrease.

Tip: You may not always find it advantageous to raise prices. You must find creative ways to increase income. As an alternative, you may do more marketing, increase product lines, add additional services, or replace/reeducate unproductive employees.

Your Business Office and Supplies

In order to maintain an efficient business, you will need a variety of office supplies. They may be used entirely at your reception desk or in a separate managers office. All payroll records, receipts and business records should be kept in the manager's file cabinet or charted on the computer. Below is a list of potential office supplies. This list is not all inclusive.

Office Supply Check List

- Appointment book
- Calculator
- Cash register (optional)
- Computer (optional)
- Envelopes
- File cabinet
- Index cards and file case
- Note paper
- Paper clips and container
- Pens and pencil
- Postage stamps
- Postcards
- Rubber business stamp and ink pad
- Sharpener
- Stapler and staples
- Telephone

Automation: Choose Your Computer

Choosing to automate your bookkeeping system could be the wisest business decision you ever make. You have at your fingertips all the information you need to assess your business's productivity. You will have daily, weekly, monthly, and yearly financial figures to keep you completely informed. Personal computers and software programs have become more affordable and easier to use in recent years.

You can choose between a Mac or a PC compatible computer. Interview all applicable companies to determine the best brand for your salon. Choose a system that is easy for you and your employees to learn and operate.

Whether your salon has three employees or thirty, there are many advantages for implementing a computer. Below is a list of available options. Please be aware that these companies may have made changes to their software since this book was written.

1. Mikal Software has software that specializes in salon management, salon marketing, day spa, beauty industry accounting and more. Reach them at www.mikal.com

2. Advantage Software: This company has software for the salon, spa, nail salon, medical spa and laser center. You can download a demo version at www.aknaf.com/salon/

3. Envision Salon and Spa Management Software is specifically for salon and spa owners to help operate and grow their business. Reach them at www.ennoview.com

4. The Spa/Salon Manager Software was designed with simplicity in mind. Software package encompasses appointment scheduling, email marketing, gift cards and payroll processing. Reach them at www.spasalon.com

Computer Disadvantages

Computers are helpful on many levels, and not everyone appreciates technology. There are disadvantages. It's time consuming to input the data. Data must consistently be input for accurate figures. Many people have a fear of computers, and there may be a high learning curve for employees. The cost of computer hardware, software, printer and any other peripherals could run into thousands of dollars. It also takes up space on the desk.

Tips and Gratuities

According to the California Department of Industrial Relations, a tip is money a customer leaves for an employee over the amount due for goods sold or services rendered. The tips belong to the employee, not the employer. The tip must be paid on the next payday after the credit card transaction and the credit card processing fee cannot be deducted from the gratuities. Tips can be shared if a shampoo person helps out a stylist. Tips and gratuities can not be considered part of an employee's "regular rate of pay."

Employees receiving $20.00 or more a month in tips should report their earnings to their employer by the tenth of the following month. You are required to keep a daily diary and deduct Social Security and Federal taxes from the money you receive from clients. This amount affects your Social Security and Medicare benefits you qualify for when you retire, become disabled or die. Use IRS Form 4070A, Employee's Daily Record of Tips.

In Conclusion

Take the time to put together your bookkeeping system. Make it simple for yourself, or if you don't feel competent turn it over to a professional accountant. When I had my salon I did my payroll manually each week, but today's computer programs do that for you. Take advantage of automation.

Notes:

CHAPTER NINE

Cash in on Other People's Expertise

You can save yourself a lot of time and money, and avoid headaches and stress by using the expertise of other professional people.

Here are four good reasons to create your own professional support team.

1. Owning and managing a small business is a gratifying experience. Managing a business is one thing, but running it successfully is another story. Simply speaking, all it takes to get a business going is a customer. But to keep it going, and to make it grow to your satisfaction requires some expertise and business skills you may not have at this time.

2. The ideal business person is a generalist who is able to lead in all areas of business, has a broad range of experience and the knowledge to solve any problem. Most new entrepreneurs do not totally qualify for this position. A business education is helpful, but most salon owners do not have this background. They acquire knowledge and experience a little at a time, mostly *on the fly* from former employers. If so, then your business skills are in BIG trouble. When challenging circumstances arise,

business owners make a spontaneous decision, which may get them into trouble. We call this *the school of hard knocks*.

3. Regardless of your educational level, the most intelligent decision you will ever make is to seek the advice of people who know what you do not have the time or the ability to learn.

4. You need a team of professional advisors to assist you in your decision-making processes. This requires a sense of balance, simplicity, intuition, and a basic knowledge of business fundamentals.

Solo, but not Alone

Cosmetology school may or may not offer your basic fundamentals in business principles. That isn't exactly their job. Their job is to teach you the technical skills to work in a full-service salon, and serve clients in the most safe, efficient and knowledgeable manner. Protecting the client from harmful chemicals is a major concern, and rightfully so. An employee can do a great deal of damage by being misinformed, in a hurry or ignorant of the processes. That is why malpractice insurance is a must in your business. Obviously, you can't know everything about accounting, taxes, and the law. Sole proprietors sometimes think they are alone in their venture. But the truth is that you are not in it alone, not unless you want to be alone.

Create Your Own Support Team

Avoid costly mistakes by having a team of well-informed advisors. These people are well-regarded professionals in their own fields. Their job is to give you enough critical and intelligent information so you can make the most informed decisions. They have the knowledge and expertise to suggest viable options.

Legalese is the language used in the business world. These are legal technicalities found in legal documents, forms and contracts. It can be somewhat intimidating to a first time business owner. Making critical and expensive decisions may be a new experience to you and at times it will appear to be overwhelming. You don't have to take unnecessary risks. Get the help of a professional who is on your team.

Every successful entrepreneur has a team of professional advisors to support his or her goals. Your personal team is not anyone your employees or clients ever see, but they are invisible partners who support you in your pursuit of prosperity and success.

Where to Look for Business Advisors

Networking is the best way to find advisors. Ask your personal and business acquaintances for recommendations of someone with whom they have had dealings, who have good credentials and satisfactory expertise. You may even have a friend or relative who can provide these services to you.

It may take some time and several interviews to find one who has a compatible business attitude. You are looking for professionals with small business experience, who can negotiate a lease, give you tax advice, help with compensation issues, insurance laws etc. You must be able to communicate effectively and achieve trust in these individuals.

Here is a list of potential business advisors:

Accountant
Salon owners who do not understand accounting procedures and tax laws will find an accountant of utmost importance. If you

have a small salon and good basic bookkeeping skills you may not need the services of a full time accountant. However, tax laws and forms can be complicated so it is helpful to have an accountant to call at tax time. Remember to keep all of your business receipts and records for the past seven years. Records will protect you in case you are audited.

Your accountant will assist you in whatever taxes your state requires you to pay. The federal government will send you a circular E form to keep you current on tax increases and decreases. Deductions are determined by the employee's marital status and number of dependents.

Implement an organized inventory system to prevent overstocking, under stocking, and establishing a net worth at the end of the year. Use your computer to maintain peak efficiency and profitability.

Records are of value only if they are correct, concise and complete. They are necessary to meet the requirements of the federal and state laws regarding taxes and employees. Records are necessary for determining profit and loss, proving salon value to potential buyers, for arranging bank loans, and for making yearly comparisons. Keep a record of employees, salaries, length of employment, addresses, telephone numbers, and Social Security numbers. Income is classified as *income from all services and retail sales.*

Advertising Agency

An advertising agency or a graphics design firm can help you coordinate your image and marketing campaign from the very beginning. Plan a budget for advertising and promotions before you call anyone. Develop your professional image early if you want your business to be taken seriously. They'll help you with a logo, signs, business cards, brochures, web site, newspaper advertisements and any other marketing needs.

Be sure to give the agency enough information about you and your business to do a thorough job. Be open to new possibilities and added direction.

Word of mouth is the best way to choose an advertising design team. If not you can call local designers or advertising agencies. View current work on their web sites and portfolio pages. Notice if their work is appealing to you and in a style you would like for your own materials. Their client testimonials should help you decide whether to go with them or not.

Attorneys

When starting your business or before making any major changes, it is always advisable to get advice from a qualified attorney. There are often legal loopholes which many people are unaware. Find an attorney who is experienced with your kind of business.

You will need the services of an attorney mainly for purchasing or selling your business or franchise, when negotiating a lease, dealing with malpractice claims, and any other legal problems.

Bankers or Loan Officers

Developing a relationship with an officer from your local bank can be a tremendous advantage. Bankers can be a source of valuable financial assistance.

Business Consultants or Mentors

A mentor or consultant is someone who has expertise in your chosen field. They've been through it all, seen it all, and can give valuable advice about doing it a better way. Look for someone you can trust, who is objective and intelligent. There are times when you won't be able to see the forest for the trees (so to speak) and will need the advice of an unbiased individual. They act as a sounding board for your ideas and assist you with inspecting the options before making a final decision.

A mentor's advice could prevent you from making a critical mistake, or assist you in moving forward in your ventures. It is equally important to use good judgment, your intuition, common sense, and your personal comfort zone when making decisions.

Distributor Salesperson

A distributor salesperson is a sales representative who presents and sells cosmetology products specifically to hair salons. They work for supply houses and sell their products to salons for a reduced price. A good salesperson will display honesty, integrity, patience, and a thorough understanding of the products they sell.

The salesperson will call on you once a week or so to take your orders and present the newest products, merchandise and tools. Your distributor salesperson provides a lot of knowledge regarding what the salon should purchase in order to run a profitable business. As a business owner, you have the right to add a mark-up price and therefore make a profit from sales to your clients.

I've personally found the distributor salesperson to be one of the most invaluable advisors you can have on your team. You see them more often then other professional advisors, usually every week, so you tend to develop more of a personal relationship. A friendly and trusting relationship is developed over time.

Tip: It is advantageous to establish a good working relationship with your salesperson. They can tell you what the hot sellers are, which products are successful or unsuccessful in other salons, the best deals to save you money, and also extend to you a line of credit. Try to allocate a portion of your time each week for your salespeople. They keep you informed between seminars and during times when you are too busy to read sales literature.

Beauty Supply Houses

There are two kinds of beauty supply companies. The first is known as cash and carry, and the other offers personal service with delivery. Many supply houses who offer cut rate prices also lack sales representatives who sell to you directly at your salon. Because their system is cash and carry, they don't have to pay extra salaries beyond stock people and cashiers. That way they can pass the savings on to you.

Other supply houses will charge a little more, but they will deliver or ship the product to your salon, show you new products and merchandise, and help educate you on those products. Only you can weigh the advantages of both.

Keep in mind that the beauty supply business can be cutthroat. Suppliers under price each other for sales, and occasionally a supply house will sell professional products directly to the public. This practice hurts salon retail sales and services.

TIP: When certain supply houses have a sale, they advertise what are called *loss leaders*. They mark down several high profile items below cost in order to attract you into the store. You eagerly purchase the sale items and realize a savings. While you're in the store shopping, you will probably purchase other products which may not be economically priced. Be cautious, because your savings may be eaten up by the higher cost of the additional products you purchase.

Win BIG with Credit

There is one BIG advantage to buying on credit with a beauty supply company. They will allow you to order your retail products at the beginning of the month without paying for them. You then have the whole month to sell the products, then pay for them at the end of the month. So, in essence, you have used the supplier's products and it didn't cost you anything until the end of the month. By this time you've sold the products, have a cash flow and received your profits.

It's very easy to charge up a large bill with several suppliers, so if you don't want to overextend yourself, paying as you go is another option. Pay by COD (collect on delivery).

Counselors and Therapists

In your quest to attain financial freedom and maintain a successful salon, you may find that other areas of your life have become stressed by the ongoing demands of day to day business. Occasional frustrations and depression often develop. Family or friends may be putting pressure on you to take time away from the salon, while you think it would fail without you. Learn to take care of your emotions and mental well-being. Talking to a counselor or therapist can help to relieve fear, isolation, and tension. Getting it all out may allow you a new perspective. It could ultimately improve your situation.

Many salon owners become stressed during expansion or remodeling of the salon. Training new employees can be another situation that may cause you some mental discomfort. Almost every salon owner experiences a troubling situation when employees refuse to work as a team or become jealous of each other. As you experience both success and failure, you may need support in coping with your feelings of anxiety and fear. You are the leader and a good mental outlook is critical. Take care of yourself.

In Conclusion

There's real value in choosing a team of advisors. They can make your business experience flow better and be much more pleasant. Your chances of making it BIG are also much better than not making it at all. You'll also sleep better at night.

Notes:

CHAPTER TEN
How to Develop a Grand Salon Image

The Oxford American Dictionary describes an image as *a representation of a person or thing, the visual expression of something in a lens or mirror.* It is the concept or general impression of a person, firm or products, perceived by the general public. There are two aspects to the idea of *salon image.* One is the physical impression or image of your salon, and the other is the visual expression of you, your management style and your employees.

You probably already have some ideas about the colors or wall coverings you want. You'll decide the type of furnishings you want: equipment and furniture, showcases, product shelving, mirrors, reception desk, posters or art, floor coverings or carpet, lighting and other amenities. It's a total package you'll offer to your clientele. Will it be a 'comfort' package, a 'luxury' package, or a 'funky' package? How will you appeal to the client you want to attract?

Reflect the Real You

Your business is a reflection of you. It's your creation and the results of your goals or dreams. Determine the physical image you want to project to the public. Are you classy and prestigious or informal and low key?

Do you have a strictly professional demeanor or do you have a *devil may care* attitude toward business? Your attitude will manifest itself in your public image, which may have an effect on your relationship with your clients. As a new business owner, you have the opportunity to begin now and express your creative talent and/or diversity.

If current salon owners want to upgrade their professional image, it is necessary to define that image first to themselves, then recreate it for the public.

Exercise: Clarify beliefs and attitude toward your profession

1. Depict the image you want to portray:

2. State your philosophy in regards to your profession:

3. Describe your philosophy regarding *your salon* in particular:

Tip: Remember, an image is not just about how you *look* to the prospective client, but also how you *feel* to them.

Design Your Image for Your Specific Market

Do you have a vision for your salon business? Is it clear and detailed to you? Can you use your imagination and step into it as if it were real? This is the time to think about how you can present your business to the public.

You can design your salon for a specific market. A nursery school environment will attract a youth market if you design your salon with specific equipment and child-related furnishings. Suitable salon colors would be bright and bold. Equipment suppliers design animal theme hydraulic chairs for the little ones. A play area with a quantity of toys is a must. Make sure the playthings you choose are safe for small children. Books, music and videos geared to children's interests would be appropriate. The stylists' could be innovative and dress in costume or wear bright colors.

A teenage-theme salon could implement music videos, popular teen music, video games and posters of pop icons. It would be advantageous to employ a younger staff and dress in trendy attire and wear the newest hairstyles.

Design an all-male salon in a masculine decor. A wildlife, sports or business theme would be appropriate for the comfort of these clients. Who you choose to hire would be an important decision in attracting and keeping an all male clientele. Male inspired art and products would round out the theme.

An older, more affluent clientele might appreciate a classy and sophisticated image with lots of personal service. Gilded mirrors, chandeliers, soft lighting, and elegant carpeting will appeal to the well-heeled guest. Purchase an upscale coffee center so clients may have their cappuccino, latte' or espresso at the push of a button. Stylists dressed in casual elegance attire will bring together a salon tailored for a king or queen.

Use your creativity and ingenuity to personalize your salon. Be a trendsetter and develop your own style. Make it a fun experience, but also be practical. Remember that it's a place of business and will attract some wear and tear.

Salon Image Exercise:

1. What style of logo will you choose?
2. What kind of signage will you choose?
3. How do you want your salon to look? What style?
4. What colors are you using?
5. What style of equipment?
6. What kind of furniture in your waiting area?
7. What kind of posters or art?

8. What is the layout or floor plan of your new salon?
9. What else is important to you?

How to Create a Positive Personal Image

There's more to a professional image than what your clients see when they walk through your door. Whether your public image is fancy or funky it is also defined by the way you present: *yourself, your salon, your business practices, and the method in which you treat your clients.* Everyone has a personal management style, whether they are aware of it or not. If you are not certain yours is positive or effective, ask for a critique from your partner, or an employee who is honest and has good judgment. Project a positive and conscientious image by practicing good business habits.

Here are a few suggestions:

1. Greet your clients and introduce yourself. Introduce the client to their stylist/service provider. Speak clearly, smile, give a firm but friendly handshake, and demonstrate a sense of caring.

2. Return phone calls as soon as possible. A conscientious business person knows that a prompt reply is always appreciated.

3. Be punctual about answering your mail, email and phone calls.

4. Paying your bills on time gives you credibility in the eyes of your business associates and avoids penalties.

5. Keep a supply of thank you notes to send clients who refer their friends.

6. Show your appreciation for any gifts you receive and acknowledge the sender in writing. This reinforces your gratefulness and establishes good will.

7. Always practice good personal hygiene. It's helpful to keep deodorant, a toothbrush, toothpaste, and breath mints on hand.

8. Punctuality is important. It reflects a sense of respect for your clients and team members.

9. Keep your salon clean, especially the bathroom. Stock plenty of paper toweling, soap, and bathroom tissue. Follow State Board rules and regulations. Keep exterior windows and doors clean, and signs freshly painted.

10. Make sure your equipment is in good shape. It should be comfortable, sturdy, and not collapse under the weight of a heavy client. Repair any torn fabric. Keep your carpet and draperies clean.

11. Organize your desk. Clear away any clutter.

12. Is your music appealing? Play music that appeals to your client's taste. Experts maintain that 'light jazz' is the most relaxing to clients. Some salon owners prefer to have no music. They aren't competing with background noise for their clients' attention.

13. Will you offer coffee, tea, soda or snacks?

Make a list of what you would do to create a positive personal image.

1.
2.
3.

Develop Outstanding Management Skills

Opening a salon isn't just about setting up your dream salon, attracting the perfect stylists and clients and taking it all to the bank. That's the good part. You are now also the manager and you'll have many obligations. Becoming an income-producing owner/stylist is a big part of the job, and you must take care of business.

Here are some duties for which you may be responsible:

- Produce the salon schedule, covering all shifts or hours.
- Monitor salon performance, set goals for each employee.
- Train new employees. Provide feedback and reviews for employees. Maintain personnel records.
- Determine pay rate, commissions, bonuses, contests, and gifts.
- Set up insurance plans, paid vacations or any other benefits.
- Hire and terminate when necessary.
- Purchase all supplies and maintain your budget.
- Purchase retail inventory.
- Conduct regular staff meetings and update/train staff on new products and services.
- Arrange for cleaning of the salon, equipment, retail areas, stock room and implements.
- Handle customer inquiries, complaints and comments.

- Place your state board license and guidelines in an appropriate location.
- Keep peace in the salon. Manage any employee conflicts in an expedient manner.
- Pay bills on time.
- Plan a marketing campaign and relate it to staff.

Tip: Some of these duties can be delegated to your salon coordinator. Otherwise you are in charge of everything.

Twelve Ways to Protect Your Image

Keep the Peace

One of the hats you'll have to wear as an independent business owner is that of a peacekeeper. Salon life can be stressful and sometimes there are conflicts among the staff and the clients. Pay attention to what is going on around you and stay aware of any potential conflicts, jealousies or miscommunications. Keep an open communication policy so your staff may feel comfortable talking with you about their issues or concerns.

Issues come up that you could never be trained for, so you must use good judgment and common sense *in the moment* to handle any adverse situations.

When you choose your staff, you'll most likely choose individuals who are much like yourself. That should present very little conflict. You can be surprised by a staff member's challenging behavior. You may need additional training to be able to handle conflict resolution.

Take care of yourself whenever your management responsibilities become more than you can handle. Make an appointment with a counselor or therapist to help you get through challenging times. It's critical that you maintain good mental and emotional health. You'll find it easier and more fun to run your salon when you are happy and peaceful.

What will you do to keep the peace?

Make it BIG by Demonstrating Competence

You must demonstrate competence in your business practices, not only to the general public and to business colleagues, but specifically in front of your employees. Credibility is important. Think of it as a present investment with incredible future effects. Have confidence in yourself and in your staff. Be creative in your efforts to stay motivated.

Be Compassionate

Compassion is an essential ingredient. We all enjoy the company of other people who listen well, are caring and warm-hearted. Seek to be helpful, kind, and understanding in all situations.

Blow Your Own Horn

Post your business license, state board licenses, policies, trophies, ribbons, and awards in a conspicuous place. These items represent the time and effort you've invested in your career.

Be Professional

Whether you have a receptionist or not, always answer your phone in a professional manner. Speak slowly and clearly. Be patient, and listen attentively so you answer the callers' questions, solve the problem or direct the response to the appropriate person. You can turn on an answering machine when you leave for the evening, but probably won't want to receive messages. It's best to be able to respond personally in order to avoid errors.

Create a Powerful Presence

Current studies claim that you have between 5 and 20 seconds to make that vital first impression. You have a brief amount of time to present yourself in a positive and professional manner. Be powerful.

Pay attention to your body language. Do you directly face people with whom you are speaking? Do you give them your full attention or does your body position say that you really have something else to do?

How is your energy level? Are you able to show enthusiasm even when you aren't particularly interested in a client's conversation? Can you be exuberant about your workload even though you're really tired? Do you have a strong work ethic?

Resist Gossip

A hair salon can be a breeding ground for gossip and rumors. Avoid the reputation of being a salon where one can hear the latest trash or scoop on you-know-who. Never repeat a rumor that could hurt someone's reputation. It's wise to stay neutral. If someone takes you into their confidence on a personal matter, you need to treat it as such. (Don't rely on your memory for all the details of your last appointment with this person.) Make sure your employees understand the importance of this policy.

Listen with Compassion

Keep in mind that not everyone will share your beliefs and opinions on beauty regiments. Yes, you are the professional, the expert, *and* you still need to listen to the thoughts of your stylists, your clients, and your salespeople.

It's important for the owner or employee to be friendly, sociable and even supportive of clients. It's not necessary to dump all your troubles on a client.

The stylist or salon employee often plays the role of therapist during services. Some clients feel confident in sharing their personal problems. I've personally had clients break down and cry during an appointment (not because of anything I did wrong, but as an emotional outlet). You are not expected to give therapeutic advice, but merely to listen, and be understanding. Respond if you feel you have something positive to offer.

If listening to personal problems is a source of discomfort to you, then you can make every effort to speak only of products and services. Take the role of a consultant, and provide the client with information pertaining to their salon service. They'll be thankful for that too.

Get an Attitude Tune-up

Be aware of when your attitude needs a tune up. It's easy to fall into the negativity trap. When you sense that you are frowning more than smiling and complaining more than complimenting, then it's time to *take a time out before you burn out*. Whenever I feel I'm in need of attitudinal healing, I attend a motivational seminar, listen to inspiring tapes, or talk to a counselor or a caring friend.

Go the Extra Mile

Be observant of your client's likes and dislikes. Make the effort to do those *extra little things* to make the client think of you and smile: order magazines that clients enjoy, purchase unique coffees or teas for their drinking pleasure, decorate with fresh flowers or have some nice snacks on hand.

Keep Accurate Records

Many mistakes occur by stylists who do not keep accurate files on hair color and permanent wave services. Keep your files up to date, and review them before and during the service. Note any changes and results. Nothing can ruin your professional reputation quicker than when you become a salon known for inconsistent services. Paying attention to details gives more value to services.

Build Your Image One Step at a Time

Building your image is an on-going task. It's like building a home. You lay down a sturdy foundation, then add one brick at a time until it's complete. It will require many hours of your time, but intensive planning in the beginning stages of your career will influence your success for years to come. Be certain that your employees understand the image you are projecting. Their cooperation is critical to your overall success.

How to Discover Trends

Learn to discover trends by developing an astute awareness for diversity. Read a variety of books and focus on trade and news magazines. Watch the news and popular television programs.

Pay attention to what celebrities and pop stars are doing. Notice what people in European countries are wearing. Attend trade shows on a regular basis. Notice what styles people on the street are wearing. Be question oriented about what is happening now: who, what, when, where, how, and why? Those questions are clues to discovering trends.

The 1980's saw a major change in the salon industry. There was a predominance of chain and value-priced salons where clients could go for quick service and a low price. Chains have been growing at an annual rate of 15%. 'Volume' was the buzz-word for the 1980's. Salons that didn't jump on the discount bandwagon or alternately progress to 'upscale' found themselves out in the cold. They had difficulty competing with the leaders. Those changes were a prime example of big business and effective management giving *mom and pop* a run for their money.

The 1990's saw a continuance of the chain salons almost to a point of saturation. But there is a resurgence of the upscale progressive salons as the consumer demands more personal attention.

"The day spa and medical spa concept have become a booming business as Baby Boomers age and require more pampering and medical anti-aging enhancements."

Professional Salons' have gained a larger share of the lucrative men's market by placing more of an emphasis on barbering techniques. Salons and stylists who became adept at clipper cutting found themselves with an additional stream of income. Men tend to be loyal to neighborhood haircutters, and get trims more often than women. Clipper cuts have two advantages: they are quick to implement once you learn the technique, and they take half the time so you earn twice as much money.

Salons that consider themselves savvy business experts are computerized in order to maintain peek efficiency and profitability. The days of casual management are over. A large number of product manufacturers have made a commitment to research and development of environmentally-friendly products and are sensitive to the concerns of global preservation. Many companies have eliminated animal testing on products, removed animal by-products, use biodegradable products and are implementing recyclable packaging for products.

Tip: Salon Owners - You now have a choice and you can make a difference. More manufacturers have taken a stand against product diversion. Diversion is selling *professional only* products to drugstores and discount stores. These products are meant to be sold only in salons where clients can receive proper instruction as to their use. Manufacturers and salons that practice diversion hurt the professional salon industry by taking away salon sales and customer education.

The leading companies have always and will continue to make a commitment to education, which in turn helps the salon industry grow.

Demographic Profile and Trends

The five types of demographics are basically: age, gender, income level, race and ethnicity. The average client is a 35-62 year old working woman who is looking for personal service. The emphasis will be on the discriminating individual and what looks good on her. The most loyal male salon-goer is the appearance conscious 25-34 year old. The progressive salon will take on the role of a *total image consulting service*.

Clients visit their respective salons an average of about 10 times per year. Clients expect high quality, a courteous staff, a clean environment, convenient hours, and reasonable prices. More salons use *professional only* or European imported products as they continue to compete with department stores, drugstores, supermarkets, and other discount outlets for a larger share of the beauty products.

In Conclusion

Your salon's physical image and your personal image coincide to make a grand expression of who you are in your community and among your business peers. These are some of the most important decisions you will ever make. It's critical that you *get it right* from the beginning.

Notes:

CHAPTER ELEVEN
Make it BIG With the Right Location

Any real estate agent will tell you the rule of thumb in choosing good real estate is location, location, location. The same rule applies when you are purchasing or renting business property. Do your market research and it will pay off BIG. Check with your Chamber of Commerce for information on population, average income, industry and business potential. You can also look on government web sites for current census data.

How to Find the Perfect Location

Before looking at rental space, refer to your business plan (Keep your target market and competition in mind), and decide how much floor space will be required. Draw a simple layout of your prospective salon, including room for your workstations, shampoo area, reception area, supply room, rest room, and any other areas such as nail, facial, and massage rooms. Is there an air conditioner and adequate electrical outlets? Remember that constantly running hair dryers will increase room temperature by at least 30%. You will also need easy access for shipments and deliveries.

You may eventually need more room for growth and expansion. Determine how many square feet you're going to need, then shop for a rental unit.

Call several commercial realtors. You should know the area you want, square footage needed, and how much rent you can afford. Realtors often know in advance which stores are going out of business or moving. They'll know which units will be available for rent in the near future. Choose several good locations, so that you'll be in the best position to negotiate a lease. If a landlord will not negotiate, you can walk away and still have a back-up location.

Take your time in finding the right unit. Once you determine who your clients (target market) are, locate as near to that geographic location as possible. A suburban location will attract clients within a 5-10 mile radius. However, the best location will be near other businesses: restaurants, supermarkets, offices, schools, and department stores.

"Consumers are attracted to areas for one-stop shopping. Seek out a busy location where there is high visibility and a steady flow of foot traffic."

Locate your business in an area where you have dense population and a high enough income bracket. Compare unit prices, and stay within your budget. Find out what amenities are included.

Enclosed shopping centers and strip malls are always a good bet, although they are usually more expensive than other locations because of the one-stop shopping. Remember you are paying for C.A.M. or common area maintenance and there is no ceiling on that expense. A shopping center or mall location can eliminate some of the costly marketing expenditures because they also do some marketing. These places are usually so high profile that you don't have to market your business as much as you would if you had a freestanding unit. If you can't get a mall location, make sure there is enough parking where you do locate, and be absolutely sure your chosen unit is zoned for your business: hair salon, spa, nail salon, boutique etc. A safe and well-lighted area is essential for evening hours. You will need space for a sign so check on zoning laws before you sign a lease.

Many entrepreneurs locate their businesses near their own residences in order to keep travel time and costs to a minimum.

To retain clients, a new owner/stylist with a large clientele will want to stay in the same area as his or her previous place of employment. Many clients will find it too inconvenient to travel to another town. Don't despair, if you are really good at your trade, clients will find you. It will just take them a little longer.

If you choose a home-based salon, you will need to look into local ordinances about the rules and restrictions. Contact your local government agency.

I know of several salons that have a very good business despite a poor location. The way to compensate is through persistent innovative marketing.

Position yourself for the future. Choose a good long-term location and you'll avoid making a costly move in your formative years. Your best bet is to choose an effective location that will bring growth and prosperity to your business.

Tip: Try to stay away from businesses where alcoholic beverages are served. You may have a problem when intoxicated clients stagger into your business and create problems.

The Advantage of Owning Your Own Property

Why pay rent when you can own your own building? Owning your own property/building in a high traffic area is the most desirable situation. Good business locations generally appreciate in value over the years. If you decide to go out of business or retire, you can either rent your space to someone else, try another business, or sell the building. You can also deduct it all off your taxes.

Buying property is unrealistic for many new entrepreneurs with limited resources. It's more feasible to rent space for five or ten years, and save money for a down payment on a commercial unit.

Use Discretion When Choosing a Location

Seek the competition first. One city neighborhood has four hair salons in a two block area. No matter how much money you think is there, it's very difficult to be successful when you locate your salon in a diluted market. You may not be able to raise prices because the competition is so near in proximity. There is also the possibility of losing employees to a neighboring salon. An angry client can merely walk next door.

Be certain that the unit in which you are interested does not have a history of failures. Sometimes there appears to be a jinxed unit, where businesses come and go much too fast. No business is ever truly successful in this particular location. Whether the reason for multiple failures is bad feng shui or bad management, you would be better off avoiding the location.

I would suggest questioning other business owners or residents in the area about safety measures: police protection, neighborhood violence, break-ins and other concerns.

Negotiating a Lease: Buyer Beware

Once you have decided on a location for your new business, it's time to negotiate a lease with the owner, landlord or management company. Negotiating a lease is something of a game. The landlord wants the most money for the least amount of furnishings. The tenant wants to pay the lowest price and get the most amenities for their money. If you are a good negotiator, you could try to do it yourself, otherwise it's best to seek legal advice.

A short-term lease of 3-5 years is advantageous for a new business. Short-term leases are good for testing the location. You can leave if you're not happy with it. Long leases are good for locking in the rent rate and if you plan to spend a great deal of money on leasehold improvements.

"Leasehold improvements are improvements you perform on a rental unit for business purposes, and are tax deductible."

They include painting, wall coverings, all floor coverings, plumbing, extra electrical wiring and outlets, lighting fixtures such as track lighting, recessed lighting, additional rooms, walls and more. When you move you will forfeit any improvement that is glued, nailed or in some way permanently attached.

Reading a lease can be very complicated especially if you are negotiating with a corporate management company. You will definitely need the services of an attorney. If you do not have one, ask a business acquaintance for the name of an attorney who has experience in negotiating leases. Have your attorney negotiate the lowest rent possible, the amount of lease years and any other amenities you might desire. Make sure you read the small print, and fully understand the terms involved.

I would recommend a clause that prohibits other hair salons from opening in the same building or mall. Always get your agreements in writing. Promises not written down are meaningless.

Every lease will differ somewhat, but listed below are some of the rules and regulations generally included in a lease:

- **Grant and term:** Who pays construction costs.

- **Rent:** Minimum rent, percentage rent and additional rents.

- Records and books of accounts: tenant's records.

- **Audit:** Their right to examine your books.

- **Utility service:** The tenants' obligation to pay utilities.

- **Maintenance of demised premises:** The tenant's and landlord's obligation to pay.

- **Alteration:** What you can and cannot change.

- **Indemnity and insurance:** The landlord and management company can dictate how much insurance you must have.

- **Exterior and window lighting:** Your obligation to provide adequate lighting.

- **Receiving, delivery and parking:** The location where you receive deliveries and where your employees must park.

- **Signs:** You must have landlords' permission and approval.

- **Assignment and subletting:** You must have landlords' permission to do so.

- **Access to premises:** The right of entry by landlord.

- **Eminent domain:** The landlord and tenants' right of

termination and obligation for restoration of rental unit.

- **Bankruptcy and solvency:** Procedures required by landlord.

- **Default of tenant:** Explains the tenants' rights and landlords' rights.

- **Advertising and Merchants Association:** You will be required to join the association, pay dues and attend monthly meetings. You may also be asked to be an officer or serve on a committee.

- **Operation and maintenance of common areas:** The common area maintenance or CAM fee will be attached to your monthly rent. You pay a percentage of the floor space in the mall according to the size of your unit. There is never a ceiling on this fee. There is also a 10% or 15% bookkeeping fee. You might also have to pay the landlord a percentage of your gross income. Check your lease and talk to your accountant about the implications of this option before you sign. It may or not be to your advantage.

You will have to pay a pro-rated share of the following items:

Lighting and other utilities, personal property taxes, cleaning, snow removal (if your area gets snow), line painting, policing the premises, holiday decorations, music and intercom systems, pest extermination, security services, the cost of landscaping and drainage, all salaries and compensation in connection with operation, maintenance and administrative costs.

In Conclusion

This chapter covered the nuts and bolts of choosing the right location for your salon business. It's a BIG decision and one that requires a lot of time and research. Carefully read over those contracts and talk to an attorney if there's anything you don't understand. Feel free to ask for changes. If you don't ask, the answer is always "no."

Notes:

CHAPTER TWELVE

How to Design Your New Salon

Designing your first salon can be both exciting and intimidating. Think it through and your plan will go more smoothly. It's beyond the scope of this book to cover every detail. This information plus the advice of a professional salon designer could assist you in making smart choices and avoiding expensive errors.

Read the information on *Chapter Ten: How to Develop a Grand Salon Image* before choosing equipment or a salon design. Do some important soul searching before making any commitments. If you still aren't certain about an appealing image, check with your equipment showrooms. They carry many manufacturers' books. Trade magazines also show new salon equipment. You'll be better prepared to see the whole picture, and move forward toward achieving your goals.

Create a Winning Business Name

Once you have made the decision to open a hair salon, you need to choose a name. The name of your salon will symbolize the entire business, define your image, and establish the salon's character.

You could name your business after yourself, using either your first or last name or both. If your business is successful, your name will be synonymous with success, but if your business eventually fails, your name will be associated with failure. This will give you negative name recognition.

Choose a name that tells your clients what your business does for its primary source of revenue. Allow the client to identify you as a place to meet their needs. Choose your name carefully, because you will most likely keep it for the duration of your career, which may be many, many years. If you are too specific and define yourself as just a haircutting salon, with a name like Just Cuts or Nice Cuts or a name that specifically pinpoints haircutting or one particular service, then you may be unable to attract clients who are looking for a full-service salon. No matter how much you advertise full-service, you will ultimately be limited by your name.

Take time to research the names currently used in your area so you don't infringe on another salon' territory. Don't confuse the public by choosing a name that is too similar to your competition.

"If you find that you love your salon name and it really works for you, consider buying a trademark so no one else can use it."

You'll need to do a trademark search to make certain the name is available. If so, you can trademark your name and/or logo and it belongs exclusively to you. You can do it yourself on the internet or contact a trademark attorney. At this writing, a trademark is around $300.00 and is good for ten years.

Hair salons often use gimmicky names such as 'Curl up and Dye' or 'Hot Headz' or 'Shear Power' or 'Heads You Win', 'Hair Today' and others. Select a name that conveys the essence of your business. Choose a name you are proud to use.

If you choose a name other than your legal personal name, you will find it necessary to file a Fictitious Name Statement. This is referred to as a DBA (Doing Business As) form. Each state or county has a certain office where you register your fictitious name. Check with your county or state legislature.

How to Choose a Sign

Keep all your outdoor and indoor retail signs in line with your image. Customizing your signage defines your salon even further by sending a message to your clients that you have a total image. Reinforce the strength of your image by including your logo and salon colors.

If you are using the services of a professional graphic designer for your logo, brochures, newsletters, direct mail etc., ask them to draw up some ideas for outdoor and indoor signage.

Before deciding on one of several images, be sure to ask yourself several important questions:
1. Is it professional looking?
2. Is it eye catching?
3. Does it give a good first impression?
4. Does it properly identify what business you are in?
5. Can it be clearly seen from the street?

If you can answer yes to all these questions, then you may have a *keeper.* Make certain your outdoor signage is large enough to see from the street. Advertising after dark is the benefit of a lighted outdoor sign. If a lighted outdoor sign is not feasible, then consider a lighted indoor window sign.

Certain product manufacturers feature and sell lighted window signs to promote their personal line of products. This is called cross-advertising and it provides strong product identity. It also invites credibility by marrying your business with professional products signifying quality and value. Displaying this kind of signage attracts product buyers to your business, and perhaps inspires them to utilize your services.

Neon signs used either in the window or within the salon are a fun way to add color and pizzazz to the salon. They can be used to direct clients to rooms or areas not immediately visible. Bold, bright neon lights strategically placed can also make a statement about your salon; perhaps a brief philosophy, purpose or mission statement.

There are options when choosing indoor and outdoor signs. For example, a salon owner whose image uses antiques or a country decor can ask local crafts people to create a suitable sign. It may be quite inexpensive. Consider art or line drawings from local artists and illustrators.

Get ideas and estimates from local sign makers. Signs are costly, depending upon size and complexity.

Remember to check with your attorney or zoning board to learn about local regulations and to determine if you need a sign permit. Expect to pay a small fee.

Use Posters Effectively

Professionally designed posters are another way of delivering a powerful message to new clients and your community. They can help you make money and be aesthetically appealing.

Hire your own attractive models and give them current hairstyles. Design small posters on your computer graphics program and place them in acrylic frames. A large poster of an attractive model strategically placed in my window got me more clients than other forms of marketing.

Evaluate Your Present Space

You may already be in business and need to renovate for a fresh new look. Before you make any costly renovations, you must provide some important information. Determine if your current space and building is satisfactory, and if it is worth what could be a substantial investment in renovations. Here are some things you may want to look out for:

1. Note when your lease expires. Is it soon or in five years? Consider that your rent may increase at that time.
2. Be aware of any positive or negative changes in your neighborhood. You may or may not want to be tied to a long-term lease.
3. If the neighborhood is growing in positive ways, you may find advantageous reasons to stay and expand your business.
4. Consider the unit structure, and how easy or difficult it will be to relocate plumbing, electrical, and add or delete walls.
5. Pay attention to remodeling restrictions in your lease. Will there be enough parking when your business expands?

How to Choose Your Salon Equipment

Your choice of equipment is one of the most important and expensive decisions. The quality and comfort level of your equipment influences how clients relate to your image.

The In's and Out's of Buying Equipment

When purchasing new or used equipment, remember to choose a style that is *in*, and stay away from old fashioned equipment that is *out*. Remember your image and try to stay within a style and price range that reflects how you want to be perceived in the marketplace.

There are several places to purchase new and used equipment. You can buy equipment from manufacturers and beauty supply distributors. Regional cosmetology shows are a good place to view and price the most current and trendiest styles.

When you purchase new equipment from manufacturers, they will often let you choose from several designs at no additional cost. Their salon designer will usually have several layouts from which you can choose.

When you purchase your new equipment, plan for the future and be certain to purchase everything you think you'll need. Eventually the manufacturer will discontinue styles and fabrics.

Make copies of the blueprints. The complete floor plan includes plumbing, electrical outlets, supply room, bathroom, etc. to send to the state in order to obtain your license (Check with your state for requirements).

Tip #1: Keep an extra set for yourself and also for the shopping center manager or mall owner.

Tip #2: I would like to make one last personal comment on new equipment. Many salespeople will try to convince you that purchasing expensive new equipment is the best way to go, and it is if you want to complete a total image. One selling point they use is "it'll last a lifetime." Whether your new equipment will or won't last a lifetime is certainly debatable. Keep in mind that after about six or seven years, styles not only go out of fashion, but can make your salon look obsolete. Hair and fashion images constantly change, so must your salon. Also, wear and tear on even the best equipment can soon make your salon look shabby. The key, I believe is to get the best quality equipment for the lowest price.

However, if you have unlimited financial resources and a vision of having the classiest salon around, then by all means *go for it.* You'll be proud and happy with your new salon.

Choose Your Styles and Colors

Choose styles and colors that reflect your chosen image. Are you interested in the influence of art deco, international, and classic looks for salon décor? Do you like the new European styles? The Italian collection emphasizes bold colors, simple asymmetrical lines, and rich ultra-modern structure.

Neutral colors always look fresh and never go out of style. You'll want to coordinate your equipment style and colors with your wall and floor coverings. Matching display units for the retail area and shelves for the supply room help to finish your total look. Choose a coordinating manicure table and stool, facial equipment and any extras at this time. Many thousands of dollars can be spent on new equipment if you want an upscale salon with a trendy image.

An interior designer can help you choose the right colors, fabrics and images for your salon. If you can't afford a designer, consider a student designer who wants the experience and portfolio pieces.

Look through manufacturers catalogs, trade magazines, supply houses and at trade shows. There you will find all the newest and most cutting edge equipment.

How to Purchase Inexpensive Equipment

You can get by rather inexpensively if start up money is tight and you are not particular about your equipment and decor. Purchase used equipment from the classified advertisements in the newspapers, on the internet or at auctions. You may be able to purchase new and used equipment on consignment from your local beauty supply distributor. Call them and ask. Remember, the same rule applies to used furniture, *you get what you pay for.*

Example: I found an equipment sale from a well known low cost beauty supply outlet. Just to give you an idea of *on sale* equipment costs, I found these options for a new salon with six stylists, and two manicurists:

- Six hydraulic chairs for $280.00 each = $1,680
- Six vanities with mirrors at $140.00 each = $840
- Three porcelain bowl/shampoo chair combinations at $590.00 each = $1770
- Two portable manicure tables for $90.00 each = $180
- Two manicure chairs for $60 each = $120
- Six stylist mats for $40.00 each = $240
- Two hair dryer/chair combinations - $130.00 each = $260
- Three supply trolleys for implements $50.00 each = $150

Total = $5,240   *(7/01/11)

In this example you get the bare bones minimum start up costs for equipment. Your investment would cost you $5,240 (more or less) just to outfit your salon with simple low cost equipment. Obviously you still need plumbing, electrical work, supplies, signs and many more items that would add to your bottom line. There is also rent and deposits.

Make it BIG by Purchasing an Existing Salon or Franchise

When you purchase an existing salon it frees up your valuable time to focus on business rather than making crucial start up decisions. Color schemes or fabrics can be changed, and furniture/equipment can eventually be reupholstered for a fresh new look. Your time and money would be better served by focusing on marketing and promotions.

The challenge with purchasing an existing salon is finding a fair price for both the buyer and the seller. Both parties want the best deal. You'll need to do a lot of research into costs, and look at the seller's financial numbers. It's best to have the assistance of an accountant. Should you decide to go with a franchise, you will be required to follow the franchisers mainstream ideas. You'll find more detailed information about franchise operations in *Chapter Four: Identify Your Business.*

Equipment Checklist

Here is a list of equipment pieces and tools to equip your salon. The amount of pieces you'll need will be determined by the size and type of your salon.

Checklist:

Ashtrays
Back-bar bulkheads
Brooms, mop, bucket, and dustpan
Coat rack and hangers
Children's booster seat
Cordless clocks
Coffee maker
Desk and rolling stool
Dressers or styling stations
Dryer chairs
Entry carpet
Facial chair
Garbage cans with lids
Hand mirrors
Hydraulic chairs
Heat lamps
Holiday decorations
Hot wax machines
Jewelry showcase

Magazine rack
Manicure table and rolling stool
Outdoor sign
Posters and wall hangings
Reception chairs
Roller carts for permanent wave rods or rollers
Shampoo bowls and tilting chairs
Showcase units for retail area
Shelving or cabinet for supply room
Table and chairs for employee lounge
Timers
Towels and shampoo capes
Vacuum cleaner
Washer and dryer
Wet and dry sanitizers

Your business telephone needs to be reserved for incoming calls. You may also install a business telephone with two or more lines so that you can accept more than one incoming call. One line can also be used for personal calls without disturbing the business line. Most people now use cell phones so that frees up all your lines for business purposes.

Purchase Your Salon Tools

The following items may be purchased entirely by the salon, or the stylists may be required to bring all of their own tools.

Checklist:

Applicator bottles
Applicator brushes
Brushes - various kinds

Blow dryers (optional)

Combs - various kinds

Curling irons (optional)

Diffusers

Electric clippers (optional)

Hot rollers

Mixing bowls

Permanent wave rods and papers: dozens of different types

Razors and blades (single edge)

Sanex strips

Spray bottles

Timers

How to Choose Good Lighting

Good lighting is critical in a hair salon, so make sure that your designers plan for enough. Fluorescent lighting is standard in most commercial units. You will pay more to have fluorescent light recessed, but it looks so much better.

Track lighting systems look trendy, and the lights make the hair appear shiny and bright. Unfortunately, it distorts the true color of the hair. The stylists in my salon would run to the lights and switch them on or off depending upon how the hair color turned out. If the hair color turned out too dark, the stylists would turn the lights on to make the hair color appear lighter. If the hair color turned out too light, they would turn the lights off. Our elderly clients would complain that the lights from above put shadows on their faces. The best light is, of course, natural light.

The most flattering light to the face are the bright bulbs which surround your mirror (the make-up mirror concept). Implement this idea in your facial area if you don't have enough natural light. Your investment could be anywhere from $500 to $1,200 per mirror.

Tip: Your track lighting system and make-up mirror lights should be put on a separate electrical line from the fluorescent bulbs. Then you can use only the lighting that you need, and save on your electric bill. For less expensive rates, purchase all of your light bulbs at a bulk rate from an electrical supply store.

How to Maximize Profits in Your Reception Area

The reception area is your first profit center and your first contact with the client. Other than your outdoor presentation (window dressings, signs and décor), this is the area where that great first impression happens. Your professional image will be expressed here more than in any other area of your salon.

- Carpeting in the reception area adds warmth and prestige.
- When choosing a desk, be certain to have plenty of room for a cash register or a computer if you use these items. Appointment books can take up a large amount of space on the desk.
- Allocate plenty of space for product displays that can be touched by the client. Let your client know you're in the retail business. Make it inviting and attractive.
- Consider seating for about eight to ten people in your reception area. The rule of thumb is to have seating for one third of the number of styling chairs. Make sure your chairs are sturdy and are made of stain-free fabric. Don't buy a love seat. Strangers won't want to sit close together. Keep your styling books and magazines in this area. Refreshments can be offered here also.
- Keep your reception area neat and clean at all times.
- Wash your windows frequently, inside and out.
- Change your posters periodically as styles change or as posters fade from the sun.

Tip: If you are a stylist-owner-manager without a receptionist, consider keeping the reception desk within your view at all times. It is advantageous to be in the position where you can keep your eye on the cash drawer.

Make Big Profits From Your Retail Area

Earlier in this chapter I talked about how the reception area is your first profit center, and *Chapter Seventeen: Optimize Retail Sales* will give you more details about this important area of your business. Sell the products you use at your back bar to your clients and you'll add BIG money to your bottom line. Many of your retail products will sell themselves, due to national advertising. You won't even have to suggest them. Your distributor salesperson will have many optional products to sell. All you need is the space and a smart looking presentation. Set up retail shelving units as space is available. Shelving units look better if they all match your décor.

"Remember the needs of your target market and choose products that are likely to be of interest to them."

Stock higher priced items like blow dryers, curling irons, flat irons, hot rollers and more. Allow clients to purchase those products and more from you rather than at department stores or mass market retailers. Other retailers are your competition in this area and there is no one trained in those stores to help consumers make decisions. You are the trained professional, and must be ready to recommend products that maintain the client's investment. That's where you have the advantage over mass market retailers who sell cheap *throwaway* hair appliances. Sell quality products that last, and clients will thank you.

Educate your staff so they are knowledgeable and secure

enough to talk about the benefits of your retail products. Set up your own training or invite a company salesperson to train your staff.

The rule of thumb is to have 2-3 full lines of products for sale. You can also have a more expensive line for clients who eventually want to move up in quality. Keep your shelves fully stocked and *never* present one or two of anything. Show that you believe in the quality and effectiveness of your products by having plenty from which to choose. If you believe in your products, your clients will too.

Retail units are generally placed in the reception area where clients who are waiting can view and study your products. You can place the units or shelves and products in front of the windows for advertising, but be aware that the sun will fade the containers and signs. Customers won't want to purchase sun-faded items, so you'll probably have to mark those products down.

How to Set up Your Shampoo Stations

Locate your shampoo area in a convenient centralized location. Stylists and shampoo employees must have easy access to this busy area. Make it efficient for the stylists to be more productive. Make it easy and quick for clients to get to, as this is generally the first stop after the client checks in at the desk. Be strategic about plumbing. There are ways to save on plumbing costs. Talk to your salon designer about placing your shampoo stations and washer/dryer in a cost effective location.

Choose shampoo chairs that are comfortable for the client as well as the stylist. My clients enjoyed a lounge type shampoo chair. They can be a bit difficult for elderly people to get in and out of, but most clients felt the comfort factor was worth the effort.

The rule of thumb for choosing shampoo bowls is to provide

one shampoo bowl for every three stylists.

The back bar will provide a place for towels, capes and neck strips. Also located here will be your shampoos, conditioners and any other quick service items. I believe most states require your towels to be in a cabinet or covered receptacle. You'll also want several covered trash receptacles in this area too.

If you purchase or have acquired cast iron bowls, they can be re-enameled when necessary. I recommend purchasing lighter colored shampoo bowls. The problem with dark (black or brown) bowls is that they are harder to clean, and abrasive cleansers can scratch and ruin the surface. Also, if you are rinsing color from a client's hair, it is difficult to see when the shampoo water has rinsed clear/clean. Check with local plumbing codes to see if a vacuum breaker is needed before ordering bowls.

Secret: You'll use a tremendous amount of water at the shampoo bowls, so I recommend purchasing a small unit from your hardware or plumbing store to lessen the amount of water that flows through the pipes (I got mine from my distributor sales person). It is easily attached onto the pipes under the sink. It can save you money on your water bill. I had three bowls in my salon, so I put it on two and left the third bowl free for full water pressure.

How to Set up the Styling Area

The styling area more than any other salon space must be highly functional. It must be attractive and instill the same image as your reception area. An efficient floor plan must be easy flowing and comfortable to salon traffic. There are some helpful ideas on the next page:

- Add a sense of expansion to a small room by placing large mirrors throughout the salon. For a more dramatic affect, choose smoky colored mirrors.
- When planning space for stylist stations, allow 125 to 150 square ft. for each stylist. A minimum of 4 ft. of aisle space is also the rule of thumb.
- Tile floors are much more practical in the styling and shampoo area than carpet. Carpet wears poorly and is not a good investment in these areas. The reception area and the hair dryer area benefit from good easy care carpeting.
- Wall vanities require less space than the cabinetry style. Choose equipment colors that coordinate with your salon image.
- Your salon colors, business cards, stationary, and brochures should all reflect a consistent image.
- You may want shampoo bowls that are in contrast with the bulkhead. Carry that theme over to the styling chairs, mirrors and stations. Coordinate your manicure table, special client seating, and rolling stools.
- If you choose neutral equipment colors, it will give you the option of adding bold color accessories. These decorative accents can be changed throughout the years when you become tired of them. It's more cost effective to upgrade to a newer, fresh look.
- Many salons now use the European style of roll about carts rather than a stationary combination cabinet/roller cart.
- It is critical that you have enough electrical outlets by each station in order to avoid appliance overload or extension cord insanity. Remember that each stylist will be using outlets for curling irons, (often more than one) blow dryers, clippers/neck trimmers, and hot rollers.
- As an extra added convenience place small attractive wastebaskets throughout the salon. Some states require

144

lidded trash receptacles. Check your state board rules before you purchase them.

Add a Chemical Services Room

If you have the extra space, you could add a specially designed area for chemical services. Many people prefer not to be seen receiving color services. A male clientele may be sensitive to being viewed by women and children. A separate well-ventilated room will provide privacy and the containment of offensive chemical odors. Include enough space for at least one styling chair, a hair dryer, a permanent wave roller cart and a shampoo bowl and chair. The minimum requirement for a chemical color and perm room is 72 sq. ft. or 9' X 8.'

Additional Rooms

You will need extra-added space/rooms for facials, pedicures, electrolysis, massage, waxing or permanent makeup. The minimum requirements are 48 sq. ft., or a 6' by 8' room. If your demand for facials is high you'll need a full time esthetician with an exclusive room. Facial equipment, beauty supplies and cosmetics consume quite a bit of space, so you'll need wall shelving and cabinets to store or display products.

Another consideration is a changing room or two where clients can change into gowns. This is especially convenient for clients who are having chemical services and prefer not to take a chance on their clothes becoming stained or smelling from chemicals. Many clients return to work after salon services and don't want hair on their clothes. A client changing room is a nice benefit if you have the space for it, otherwise the bathroom is sufficient.

Inspect your changing rooms periodically for cleanliness. Install a mirror, clothes hooks and easy to use locks. You may also want to include a chair or bench for handicapped individuals.

Set Salon Hours

Year ago, many salons were open only five days a week, and were closed on Sunday and Mondays. In the light of today's competitive market, many salons offer their clients the convenience of Sunday, Monday, and late night hours. If you are paying a high price for rent, get as much revenue from your salon as possible. The rent is the same whether you are open five days or seven. You might even consider a shift arrangement, so your employees will be fresh and not burned out by too many hours.

Staying open more hours does not always bring in more profits, although sometimes it does. You must determine if the costs of keeping the salon open longer will pay your overhead, electric and wages. You could attract more clients through neighboring businesses who attract late night or very early morning clients.

> **"Pinpoint the hours in which your salon accumulates the most appointments and sells the most retail products."**

These hours could be before 9:00 a.m. or after 5:00 p.m., depending on where you are located and if your target market is comprised of working adults. You may attract a more varied clientele by extending your hours. Choose expanded hours if your salon is located in an area where residents work a swing shift or attend college classes. Certain holidays such as Christmas, New Years, Easter, and Mothers' Day may require longer working hours.

Be sure to advertise your new hours, and take this opportunity to do additional promotions. You are *providing a convenience* and *catering* to the client. Change all signs and advertisements. Remember to tell your regular clients about the additional hours. If you are not certain that the change will be profitable, you may consider changing your hours on a trial basis for a few months, then put money into advertising it further.

Tricks: Encourage your employees to schedule permanent waves or expensive color services during slow/dead times or weekdays. Fridays and Saturdays, which are traditionally busy, will be available for quick services such as haircut and blow-styles, styling, or wedding parties. I was busy all week when I learned to shift my appointments in this way. You don't have the pressure of squeezing everyone into limited appointment times. Your BIGGEST profits come from having your salon heavily booked *everyday single day*. Your value to the business community will increase dramatically when this occurs.

Client Files

Client files serve three purposes: record-keeping, the Internal Revenue and to keep you informed of your clients needs. It's always a good idea to ask where the client heard about your salon so you know *where to focus your advertising*.

When seeing a first-time client for chemical services, be sure to do a thorough interview. Ask about previous chemical services, which products were used and what results were achieved. Also ask what medications they use.

Ask employees to write specific notes for each client's service. The information will assist a substitute stylist if the previous stylist is on vacation, ill, or busy when the client returns.

Encourage every employee to review the client's files before each chemical service so that it is implemented with foresight.

If you offer tanning services, you will need to keep track of which medications your clients use. Keep in mind that some may conflict with the tanning process.

Create a Supply Room and Employee Lounge

Rental units are not inexpensive, so floor space needs to be allocated according to its profit potential. Many smaller salons combine the supply room with an employee lounge for staff to rest or a combination kitchen for preparing and eating meals. Salons with more available floor space include an employee lounge away from busier areas. Due to the stressful nature of this business, employees need a room to relax during slow times or to just get away from the bustling salon environment. If you have the space, I recommend a relatively quiet place for your employees to go for privacy. It's one of those 'it would be nice to have' rooms.

The supply room should always be conveniently located to the shampoo area. Keep all back bar supplies here, and everything for chemical services: tint bottles and tubes, canisters of bleach, various strengths of peroxide, hair straighteners, and your supply of permanent waves and more. Your permanent wave carts could be stored here when not in use. Consider adding a sink to this area. It could be used to clean used applicator brushes, containers, combs, brushes and perm wave rods. I also placed my washer and dryer in this area.

If you use this area as a kitchen and resting place for employees, they could use the sink to clean up their dishes and cooking utensils here. An employee kitchen often includes a table and chairs, a microwave oven or a toaster oven, coffee or tea pots and supplies, cooking utensils, and ceramic, plastic, or paper cups. Either keep the coffee and tea pots in the kitchen and let your staff or attendants serve the beverages or set up a self-serve refreshment table for your clients.

I purchased a small waist high refrigerator and kept a supply of cold beverages inside. The coffee maker, supplies, and snacks were conveniently located on top as a self-service amenity.

Remodel Your Secondhand Salon

Did you buy a used salon? If so you may want to remodel it to appeal to you and your clientele. One day you may look around your salon and become aware that it's starting to look out of style, or just plain shabby. You are in the image business where appearance means everything. When your salon is in need of updating start looking for ways to refresh its image. New paint, tile or posters are a good start.

Plan well enough ahead and budget enough money to purchase everything you need. Do it once and do it right. You can be as elaborate as you want, or you can freshen up your decor and equipment inexpensively, but by all means continue to make it the best it can be.

A salon which projects a successful image to the public gains credibility by wearing and using what they are selling. You are basically in the hair care business, so you wouldn't want your hair stylists to wear out of date hairstyles. You want them to wear and sell the current look. You also wouldn't want your manicurists to have ugly, chewed up fingernails. They should be a demonstration of the best your salon has to offer.

Do your best to project an overall image that signifies quality and purpose. To be considered professional, you must give the impression that all aspects of your business are congruent.

The four advantages of remodeling can be well worth the expense, effort, and inconvenience.

1. Whenever I repainted my salon and refreshed the accessories, I noticed that my client's morale improved. Clients enjoy and appreciate going to a fresh and nicely designed salon. They're

more likely to tell their friends about a salon that radiates dignity, respect, and professionalism.

2. A newly remodeled salon can also be advantageous in recruiting employees. Stylists also prefer to create in an attractive and desirable workplace. One can be inspired to do and be their best by surrounding themselves with an atmosphere of creative possibilities. An attractive salon increases productivity and aids in the retention of staff. It may also lower staff turnover.

3. Remodeling can contribute to an increase in business revenues. Statistics report there is generally a 20% gain after the first year of remodeling. Once your old equipment is fully depreciated, you have less deductions and pay more taxes.

4. You will also have the advantage of new tax deductions by purchasing or leasing new equipment. When you consider all of the advantages, you may come out ahead by purchasing new equipment and furniture.

The disadvantages of remodeling your salon

The disadvantages of remodeling your salon are really quite obvious. If you close your salon during remodeling, you will temporarily lose revenue and new clients. Your employees may protest unless they planned their vacations at this time.

If you remain open you must prepare yourself, your employees and your clients for the inconvenience. Remodeling can be quite disturbing due to the mess, extra noise, and added construction personnel.

Use a partition to section off the remodeled areas. Post signs and appeal to the patience and understanding of your clients. Reassure everyone that the inconvenience will be brief and worth the aggravation.

There are many things to consider when deciding to remodel. Extra cash or a loan may be required to make the purchases you need. You may want to remodel during a slow season when business drops off and new clients aren't being generated. Employees often take vacations during slow periods, so that might be an appropriate time to remodel.

Salon equipment is updated usually every three to five years or so. Styles and colors change according to current trends in the marketplace.

Leasing equipment will allow you to upgrade more easily, where purchasing may lock you into a particular salon design for a while. Think it through before you act.

A Remodeling Checklist

Below is a remodeling checklist used with permission from Belvedere™ Salon Equipment.

1. What is the total square footage of your space?

2. Outer walls (brick, cinder block, sheet rock)

3. Water heater (gas/electric.) Gallons?

4. Electrical service (amps)

5. Air conditioning servicing your area (tons/BTUs)

6. Is the front entrance a double door?

7. What kind of rear door?

8. Present flooring _____ What do you want?

9. Are there columns in the middle of your space?

10. What kind of ceiling do you now have?

11. What kind of lighting?

12. Are there adequate restrooms? How many will you need?

13. What is your remodeling budget?

14. How much money will you spend per station?

15. Are you remodeling the reception area? _____
    How many people must your waiting area seat? _____
    How many people at the reception desk? _____
    Will there be a computer at the desk? _____
    A cash register? _____
    Storage space needed in reception area? _____
    Do you want a retail displays in reception? _____
    How much retail product (lines) must it hold? _____
    Is a jewelry case required? _____
    Are you going to have a make-up area? _____
    Will a tester area be required? _____
    How many changing rooms will be needed? _____
    How many people at the reception desk? _____
    Will there be a computer at the desk? _____
    A cash register? _____
    Storage space needed in reception area? _____
    Do you want a retail displays in reception? _____
    How much retail product (lines) must it hold? _____
    Is a jewelry case required? _____
    Are you going to have a make-up area? _____
    Will a tester area be required? _____

How many changing rooms will be needed? _____

16. Are you remodeling the styling area?
    A. What percentage of cut/blower work? _____
    B. What percentage of roller set work? _____
    C. How many stylists? Men____ Women_____
    D. How many hair dryers? Processing _____
        Natural_____
    E. Will a color/tint area be required? How many stations?

17. How many shampoo bowls? Built-ins ___ Exposed_____

18. Are you remodeling a manicure area?
    A. How many of each style? _____
    B. Space needed for each table? _____
    C. Will you do airbrush work? _____

19. Are you remodeling a pedicure area?
    A. Where will it be located?_____
    B. Will there be a separate wet area?_____

20. Waxing required? #___Location_____

21. Facials required? #___ Location ____ Wet_____

22. Massage required? #___ Location _____ Shower____

23. Tanning required? #_____

24. Will you have a dispensary?_____
    A. Washer/Dryer? Size_____
    B. Lounge? #_____
    C. Storage needed? How much_____
    D. Other _____

E. Other _____

F. Other _____

G. Other _____

25. Will you have a private office? ___ Dimensions_____

26. Restrooms needed? ____ Size of each?_____

In Conclusion

As you can see from reading this chapter, designing your new or secondhand salon can be a complicated matter. You must take time to think it through by not only planning for what you need in the present, but also for future growth. You don't want to outgrow your salon floor space within the first two years in business. Leasehold improvements such as plumbing, electrical and extra rooms are expensive, so you want to get your money's worth for your investment.

Notes:

CHAPTER THIRTEEN
Standard and Complimentary Services

A critical decision at the start up phase is which services will you offer? You must weigh the pros and cons of choosing a large or small start up location. Know that choosing a small, economical rental unit will limit the services you can offer and the amount of employees you can hire. A larger floor space will allow you more room for additional services, but the rental cost might be prohibitive. You must determine whether your business could survive until the extra services are paying for the extra floor space. Your research into your ideal location, target market and competition should give you a clue.

Choosing Right Services

Take stock of these ideas:
- You will appeal to a wider audience if you offer more services. Consumers enjoy the convenience of one-stop shopping. What new services can you add that don't break the bank?
- Consider the proficiency of your employees. Adding a facial room, a manicure station, or a massage room may mean hiring additional staff. The real question is whether

you have the clients or can get the clients to support the new services and expanded staff? One new service could expand your clientele.

- Convenience sells. Offer a 'no appointment' policy. You will attract the impulsive clients, and those who are in a hurry. Men tend to be impulse buyers. Can you develop one of your stylists as a barber/men's aficionado? Or a children's haircutting specialist?

- What are the newest money making opportunities? Every year there are new money making opportunities to incorporate into your salon format. You will learn about them at trade shows, and through suppliers. Be first, not last to be daring and innovative.

Tip: It's a good sign when your creativity or innovation is the talk of the town.

Tip: Install a sign that reads *all services guaranteed*. It means you believe in the quality of your service and stand behind it at all times.

Below is a checklist of typical salon services. Standard services are in bold, complimentary are unbolded text:

1. **Haircuts**
2. **Blow-drying**
3. **Roller sets**
4. **Curling irons sets**
5. Braiding (French, corn row etc.)
6. **Conditioners**
7. **Hair color: tint, bleach, highlight, henna, color rinse, touch-up and more**
8. **Various permanent waving techniques**

9. **Hair straightening**
10. Eyebrow coloring
11. **Manicures**
12. Sculptured nails, extensions, nail tips, nail wraps, French tips and more
13. Pedicures
14. **Waxing services:** eyebrow arch (wax and tweeze), chin and lip, face, legs, neck, back, arms, chest and threading
15. Facials and make-up application
16. Wigs, hair pieces, and hair extensions
17. Spa services: body scrubs, various types of massages, hot tub, wet and dry sauna, baths and more
18. Medi-spa: laser liposuction, skin resurfacing, laser hair removal and more.
19. Wigs and hair extensions
20. Classes to help clients apply make-up, use a curling iron, put on a wig or anything else they ask for
21. **Wedding day services**
22. A light lunch for clients who spend more than a couple of hours at your salon. You could order salads or sandwiches from a nearby restaurant at an additional charge.

Tip: Clients are always looking for new and innovative ways to improve themselves, whether it be their appearance or their morale. You can position yourself in the community as offering *look good* and *feel good* products and services.

Complimentary Services

Take advantage of your captive audience, and extend your salon's appeal by widening your range of services. If you have the space and financial resources, you can add extensive services to your salon menu such as the following:

Influence Clients with Apparel and Boutique Items

Open a fashionable clothing boutique. A clothing store or boutique is a natural extension of many hair salons. If you have enough extra space in your salon and the additional financial reserves, you could offer several clothing lines/and or shoes, belts, hats, handbags, scarves, jewelry, fragrances and more. There is no limit to the inventory available to you. Clients are making their personal purchases somewhere, so why not with you? It can be a fun way to expand your interests and engage your clients to come around more frequently.

You would need plenty of space to exhibit your fashion items. Include a couple of dressing rooms, and a place for inventory, bags, boxes and displays. A fashion boutique could be as simple or as complex as you care to make it. Because it is an entirely separate business from the hair salon, it would be advantageous to write your goals, mission statement and business plan as previously done. Remember that it is necessary to recruit, select, train, and manage additional managers and employees.

There is a potential challenge with mixing various businesses under one roof. The aromas from chemical services can be obnoxious. You don't want perm, hair color and nail service smells to get into your clothes. You might need a door to separate these areas from each other, or separate your boutique from the salon. This means you might also need a separate entrance to the boutique. Check with an architect before making a decision.

You'll buy your clothes at the *Apparel and Clothing Trade Shows.* Look on the internet for where these shows are located.

There are vast differences between the fashion industry and the salon business. It demands knowledge of the fashion market and buying principles. Before you take any steps in this direction, get some education or seek assistance from your advisors and perhaps a mentor who previously owned a fashion boutique. They could provide you with some invaluable knowledge.

Karen Storey, a Fashion/Clothing Store Consultant who owned two women's clothing stores (Gamine and Lobelia) and a children's clothing store (Jellybeans) in Berkeley, CA offers us some pertinent information. Learn the inside scoop on what it takes to make a clothing store successful and her coveted advice for outfitting your prospective store as a compliment to your hair salon.

"If you are interested in adding the sale of clothing to your salon: I say go for it! Women love to buy clothes. A small store is successful if it meets the needs of the surrounding community. People don't buy out of charity. They buy when it's a pleasant experience and if the product proves to be useful and satisfying. Those key elements cause them to return. I could break *the success factor* down to convenient location, competitive prices, unique products, friendly service and attractive atmosphere. The important thing is to attend the trade show knowing what brands you want to buy. The best plan is to copy, copy, copy a successful store, maybe in a different town.

The key to a successful small shop: Capitalization! I've observed which small stores survived in Berkeley over the last 40 years, and they are not those that started on a shoestring. You have to be able to pay yourself and your bills even during hard times when you're not making any profit. Over time business returns, but if you can't make it when the economy is bad, or you have a break-in, or they tear up the street in front of your shop, or here, when we had the earthquake, then you have to close. I suspect you need about six months' reserve funds to support yourself, assuming the shop can break even.

I've found that ladies even like things to be a little informal, so they think the clothes are special and unique: call it a "pop up store" and you don't even need real dressing rooms, just a shower-curtain arrangement with some nice curtains.

These are my ideas for successful buying. Get several of their basics:

Tees sell most, then knit tops, then sweaters. Don't even try to sell pants, just have a token offering. Women hate to try on pants. Don't bother with accessories. They only sell when marked down to half price and are just there for decoration. A few cheap straw hats can be thrown in for excitement and to complete the look. Don't over-buy one style. Buy only one color unless it's really a basic tee. Moderate priced lines sell better though they're harder to find.

Fashion boutiques have a downside too. The two most frustrating are the people who shoplift and the credit card companies that make so much money from each sale." *Karen Storey, April 2011*

Innovate with Computer Imaging

The concept of computer imaging is built upon the premise that in an age of technology awareness, this unique system will give your salon a technological advantage over your competition.

Start-up costs for computer imaging can be costly depending on the complexity of the equipment you choose to purchase. The initial investment makes it the most expensive salon tool: computer, software, printer, digital camera, photographic paper, and CD's with new images.

The scope of these systems has increased throughout the years. If computer imaging continues along the same path, it may prove to be a standard feature in the *Salon of the Future*.

An Image Marketing Tool

A computer imaging system is an innovative marketing tool that has the potential to become a valuable part of the salon menu. It is directed mainly toward female clients who have the greatest potential for utilizing high cost chemical services. This creates more high volume sales and larger profits. The system also includes styling choices for your male clientele as well. For the sake of simplicity, the following information will be directed toward female clients rather than using he/she terms.

Just like other salon tools used daily to increase productivity, the computer imaging system takes the guess work out of style and color choices. It solves the problem of the client who fears change. Many clients cannot visually perceive of themselves with a certain haircut, a permanent (curly or wavy hair) or a different hair color, so they avoid any services which appear as a threat to their personal comfort zone. Blonde or auburn colored hair or soft curls are abstract terms to many clients. They want to be assured that the decisions they make, pay for and must live with will serve them in a positive way.

The Imaging Process

The computer imaging system presents the client with a personal photograph of how she will appear in the future. Essentially what happens is this. A trained employee photographs the client, and her face is transported to the computer screen. On her computerized image you are able to superimpose hundreds of hairstyles and hair colors which are available in the system. She can then preview her potential *look* in advance of receiving it. So there are no surprises and presumably no mistakes. The look she chooses is saved in the system's memory bank. A comprehensive comparison and selection can be made when all of the options have been viewed. The client's new images are output on a printer as a color photograph. Now that she knows exactly how she will appear in a chosen style, she can take the photographs home to contemplate with family and friends.

Advantages of Computer Imaging

Since the client is empowered by her newfound knowledge, she can ultimately make an informed decision based on facts. Once a decision is made, she presents the photo to her hairstylist for implementation.

While viewing styles on the computer monitor, the stylist or other imaging professional explains to the client that a haircut or chemical service will support and enhance the style they have chosen, regardless of the texture, thickness or color of their hair at the present time.

1. Boosted sales and increased profits are acquired not only from selling the service of computer imaging, but also from the purchase of *additional* services and products.

2. It solves the problem of clients who have trouble communicating their desires, and of stylists who either aren't listening, have their own agendas, or are unable to mentally visualize the client's instructions.

3. Computer imaging aids the client in a more successful way by revealing to her an exact replica of her desired look. Whether the client's stylist is performing the consultation or merely aiding the client and a trained employee, communication is profoundly enhanced and the salon's chance of retaining that client is greatly increased.

Tip: Styling books assist the client to a certain degree, but are not fool proof. They can literally communicate a particular style if that style is truly what the client wants. Some clients will say they want a cut or style that they see in a photograph, but what they really desire is to look exactly like the model, which is unrealistic. Therefore, you must question the client to determine what exactly it is that they want.

Model Selection

One particular computer imaging system (which was purchased as a franchise business) included a camera, a monitor, a keyboard, a digital sketch pad with pen, and a printer. You must also purchase the software program, photographic laser paper, and eventually ink cartridges. Training is also provided.

In another model I investigated, the computer system acts as a product consultation system as well.

"Beyond exposing the client to a variety of hairstyles and hair colors, clients have the opportunity to receive an in-depth beauty consultation with visual information."

The imaging professional incorporates personal data to properly evaluate the client's individual features such as face shape, skin tone, color level, lifestyle and fashion preferences into a client recommendation chart.

Once the client's lifestyle and fashion profile are determined, appropriate options are recommended.

The printer prints out a *hair care prescription*, which summarizes the consultation and lists hair care products necessary to maintain the newly chosen hairstyle. The printed analysis includes the client's face shape, skin tone, lifestyle, hair type, and requirements for shampoo, rinse, and conditioning treatments. Also included is a prescription for daily maintenance. The client may then purchase the recommended products before leaving the salon. Check with your local beauty supply distributor to determine what products and prices are currently available.

The Challenge with Computer Imaging

The only challenge for the stylist is to successfully execute the chosen services and sell the recommended products. To effectively ease the stylist's job and satisfy the client, you need these skills: A good technical background, common sense, a photograph and a prescription.

Computer imaging is a fun and informative experience for both the trained employee and the client. Manufacturers suggest that the systems are simple to operate. On-site training sessions are offered.

The Complete System

The interactive consultation system I investigated came complete with the computer, monitor, a digitized pen, printer, software and a cabinet to contain all of these items. You can purchase the combination Computer Imaging System/Consultation Program outright or a lease to purchase option is available. Shipping and applicable state taxes are extra.

Also included was a one year warranty on all parts and labor, an 800# technical support program, and the first four hairstyle up-dates. This company provides a one day initial training and a training video. In order to promote your new imaging product successfully, you receive a marketing starter kit with ad slicks, marketing ideas and strategies.

Exercise: What are your first ideas of what you might need in the way of a computer imaging system?

Tip: No matter how attractive this unique tool appears to be, I strongly suggest that you do some research first to verify your salon's and client's needs before spending a great deal of money. It could be a wonderful investment or it could be an expensive mistake. Information can be found through the manufacturer or your distributor sales representative. Find out what your options are, then make every effort to interview salon owners who are using a system before you purchase one.

Start a Wig Center

Clients who want a new look may try on human hair or synthetic wigs and hairpieces. It's a fun, economical, temporary and non-committal way of looking different. The use of wigs are only partially effective in displaying how a client will appear in a particular hair color or style. Because wigs are generically made and have a tendency to be extremely thick, wigs appear unnatural to most clients and can be a deterrent rather than a motivational tool.

Clients like the diversity of wigs: color, style and ease of use. Wigs are a good way to add more money to your bottom line, especially if you serve a niche market. You'll need extra space to display them and a storage location.

You'll make money on the sale of wigs and also on cutting them specifically for the client's face and body size. Human hair wigs are profitable in that they need to be regularly cleaned and styled.

Women who are cancer victims and receive chemotherapy treatments buy and wear wigs until their natural hair grows back.

You can find wig outlets on the internet or from your distributor salesperson.

The Benefits of an Ear Piercing Center

Establish an ear piercing center in your salon for another inexpensive and attractive way to attract new clients and offer existing clients an additional service. You won't find a more low overhead sideline business. The tools take very little space: a drawer in which to place the piercing gun, starter earrings and a marking pencil. Ear piercing and the purchase of earrings are basically impulse-oriented.

A good inexpensive place to advertise ear piercing is in a high school or college newspaper. Add a sign in your window to attract impulse business.

You can purchase attractive professional looking displays of various styles and colors of earrings and offer them for resale. You may also want to promote your local artists by carrying artisanal earrings. Additional profits can be earned by retailing antiseptic lotions.

Tip: In order to avoid infection, the newly pierced ears must be kept immaculately clean for at least 4-6 weeks.

Hair Accessories as a Profit Maker

There is a wide array of hair accessories available:
- Simple pony tail holders or decorative rubber bands
- Barrettes and hair combs
- Decorative plastic and woven materials
- Silk flowers
- More expensive formal and wedding style hair ornaments
- Trendy hats

Again, these are impulse items. Provide styles that appeal to your youth oriented market. If you cater to the wedding market you may find it profitable to carry several varieties of silk flower headpieces.

Be HOT Stuff: a Tanning Bed or Booth

Many salons make a nice profit from tanning services. It's virtually effortless if you have the extra finances for starting a tanning business. Your salon would need an extra room for a tanning bed or you could purchase a stand-up booth. Your receptionist or salon coordinator would make appointments, and familiarize the client with the process. That person would also spray/sanitize the bed after each client. Appointments could be made on the same appointment book as other salon services.

Retail items such as tanning lotions, creams, and skin conditioners could also provide extra profits. Add an attractive display of sunglasses at your retail counter for impulse shoppers.

Trade magazine and trade shows offer many options for the tanning bed business.

TIP: Protect yourself with a release form for all clients, and especially those who take medication.

Stimulate New Business with Workshops or Open Houses

Workshops (for hair, skin, and nail care) require organization skills, but could be a good way to attract and serve potential and existing clients. You are basically educating the client on technique as well as selling products and future services. Consider an image consulting class for business women or women on the go. Possibilities are hair care (curling iron and flat iron techniques), make-up, fashion tips and health care. Serve a beverage and snacks with light music and you have an attractive event.

Charge a large or small fee for the workshop or you may allow it to be complimentary. It's a good way to stimulate business for employees who are still in the developmental phase.

Make BIG Money with Massage and Spa Treatments

Massage, esthetician services and day spas are excellent ways to increase profits. You could make your massage/spa packages as partial or complete as you like depending on your floor space. An extra room or two would need to be either incorporated into existing space or built onto your unit.

Offer therapeutic massage as a relaxing new addition to salon services. Your overhead would be at least $1,000 and up depending on quality factors. Utilize an unused room, one which can be heated if necessary. It could be costly to build out and add a room. However, the income generated from having a massage service could more than make up for the additional building costs. Do your research before moving forward.

You need these items:
1. Stationary or portable massage table
2. Rolling stool
3. Portable heater
4. A closet or hooks to hang clothes
5. A dozen or so single sheets, pillow cases and a blanket
6. Pillows and bolsters
7. Massage oils or creams
8. CD player
9. A few spa CD's with ambiance music
10. Items to retail
11. Hire a certified or licensed massage therapist

There are many benefits to having a massage service in your salon. Clients are comfortable with getting massages and often get them several times a month. You would have those repeat customers. Promote various types of massage and it increases the value of this service.

Esthetics as a Profit Center

Salons have been traditionally slower in implementing this dollar-laden market. Skin care can require a sizable investment. A skin care center with professional products, education and promotion is an investment which can pay off. Although skin care doesn't follow the fashion trend characteristic of hairstyles, there are certain market trends in which to consider.

Sun damage and skin care has become an issue of critical concern to health conscious individuals. Skin protection products will continue to be developed and refined in response to the demand. BIG profits can also be made from a display offering fashionable sunglasses.

Use the same massage room during off hours for light esthetician services. You would need to purchase some additional supplies and equipment. Your investment varies, depending on the extent of your equipment. You may also need a sink, storage cabinet and display shelves.

Various spa services could be added: facials, waxing, make-overs, permanent make-up, color analysis, and hair removal. Retail items such as creams and ointments could be sold to clients.

Day Spa Services

Many salons expand to include day spa services. It is beyond the scope of this book to discuss the many details of a day spa or medical spa. They can be a complicated business, requiring more personal service and an additional investment of time, money, staff, and absolute cleanliness. Days spas include different services depending on floor space and costs: massage, facials, microdermabrasion, chemical peels, pool, Jacuzzi, showers, wet and dry sauna, resting areas, changing rooms and more. You can make it as simple or as all encompassing as you like.

You must be certain that the area in which you are located

can support a day spa. A day spa can add a significant cost to your salon and also significant profits. I recommend taking these steps first: educate yourself about spas, and have a serious talk with current owners of spas, your current clients, your banker, and your accountant. When you are satisfied with your answers, feel free to move forward with your dream of spa ownership.

* Check with your local ordinances for the rules on massage therapists and estheticians before proceeding.

Tip: These are just a few of the extra services you could add to your salon. Many of these ideas are rather easy to start up and others are more costly. Advertising helps to promote extra services, but so does word of mouth.

Secret: Productivity and profits increase when your receptionist promotes services over the telephone and your employees speak out freely of the benefits.

Create a Beauty Supply Center for BIG profits

Go beyond your small retail area by opening a beauty supply center. It is a natural extension of a hair salon business. Profits grow quickly once clients are conditioned to purchase products from your beauty supply center. If your salon is located in a highly populated area where foot traffic is heavy, you can expand your retail area to include a larger variety of hair, skin, and nail care products and merchandise. Unused space can be turned into a major profit center. Profits from retailing could pay for much of your overhead.

Beauty supply centers are located in the front unit to attract passersby. The window is used to advertise products and special sales. A clean, attractive and well-stocked product area can be an invitation to customers who might potentially use salon services.

You'll need lots of shelf and display space to showcase your retail items. Posters and Point of Purchase displays are easy ways to promote new items.

You'll also need a cash register and credit card technology if you don't already have it for your salon.

Maintenance Requirements

There is very little maintenance required in a beauty supply center other than occasional dusting and floor cleaning. With adequate promotion, you'll find that products and merchandise sell themselves, so you aren't necessarily dependent upon the sales expertise of your stylists.

You'll need a salon coordinator or an employee to talk up the products, price and stock inventory, dust the merchandise and answer questions. Your computer program should be able to track inventory. Your regular accountant or bookkeeper would keep track of both businesses. One desk is used for both parts of your business: hair salon and beauty supply center.

How to Stock Inventory

Beauty supply stores generally choose one of two ways to stock their inventory. They might stock many lines of product with fewer quantity of each. This would give potential clients a broader range from which to choose. Products with various price points would appeal to a larger market.

Some supply centers choose fewer product lines with more quantity. The advantage of fewer lines is that you can carry more quality items, which will attract a more upscale buyer. This type of supply center would be better able to promote your exclusive private label merchandise. Sell a variety of related salon merchandise as well as jewelry and cosmetics. The choices are unlimited.

171

Selecting Products

You must decide also whether to sell retail chemical products such as hair color, permanent waves, straighteners and related items. Hair salons do not normally sell chemical products to clients, for obvious reasons, but they can be sold only to licensed cosmetologists. I'm not in agreement with selling chemical products in a salon/supply center environment. You want your clients to buy those services from you, not go home and do it themselves. But if you choose to retail in this way, you must supply a wider range of products, such as hair rollers, clippies, shampoo and haircutting capes, cutting shears, peroxide, bowls and brushes, permanent wave rods and end papers, and so much more. You have much more incidental inventory to deal with and not that much more profit potential.

How to *Do* the Supply Business

Business people who open beauty supply houses as an individual entity traditionally sell *wholesale only* to licensed cosmetologists. They have salespeople who call on local salons either by phone or in person. Orders can also be faxed. This way of doing business adds much more complexity to the nature of your business. It lends itself better as a separate business entity. However the potential may be great if you are the only beauty supplier in your town and can sell to other salons and make a profit.

The industry has expanded in the last thirty years or so and many supply houses now sell directly to the public. Some sell chemical products only to licensed cosmetologists and some make no differential. Clients who do not know their products must guess as to what products to purchase. There is often no technical expertise at the store.

One advantage to maintaining a beauty supply center is

that when you purchase your product in bulk, the cost becomes increasingly less. You could pass on the savings to your own hair salon. It is considered cost-effective management.

This is a major business decision which could become rather costly to start-up. I recommend networking with your distributor salespeople before making any decisions. Perhaps they could supply you with enough information to make an informed decision.

Continue to build your retail area until it becomes so large and in demand that it requires its own facility.

Secret: You may want to confer with your accountant first. They may have experience with this kind of business and can aid you in your decision to expand your present business or develop an entirely separate entity. They count the beans, so they have the knowledge you seek.

Open a Beauty School

There is always a demand for small beauty schools, offering students more personalized attention.

Setting up your own beauty school is another interesting alternative. Beauty schools require a larger floor space, more salon equipment, and supplies. You'll also need licensed and trained instructors. The cost and regulations for a start up make a beauty school appear prohibitive. Some of the advantages of owning a beauty school are a steady stream of well-trained employees, and the lower prices incurred by purchasing products and supplies in bulk. It is beyond the scope of this book to supply beauty school information. Your state board would be the place to call or write for additional information. Consider interviewing a cosmetology school owner to understand the pro's and con's of this business.

If you have the resources, opening your own beauty school would allow you a steady flow of specially trained employees. There is always a demand for small beauty schools, offering students more personalized attention.

In Conclusion

The sky's the limit when it comes to adding products and services to your salon menu. It's always best to do your research first before adding expensive complimentary services such as Spa or the inventory for an enlarged beauty supply area. Keep economic factors in mind when planning a BIG investment

Notes:

CHAPTER FOURTEEN
How to Price Your Services

Once you have chosen your services you will need to set an appropriate fee structure and think through an *increase* strategy. Be certain that your fee structure is credible by comparing your prices with your competition.

Service prices will vary depending upon many factors: location, overhead costs, and type of salon. You will have fixed costs such as rent, utilities, phone, equipment, maintenance, insurance, licenses, advertising, and staffing to incorporate. There will also be other expenditures such as office supplies, hospitality supplies, free samples, Christmas gifts to clients and more. All of this and more must be taken into account.

Set Your Fee Structure

Devise a strategy that is fair and appropriate. Inform your clients of a fee hike about a month or so in advance. You are in business to serve the public and to make a profit. A value-priced salon always keeps its prices low, no matter what. It depends on volume rather than higher prices.

A home-based salon, a strip mall salon, an enclosed mall salon and a downtown location may all charge different prices according to their overhead, or it's possible they may all charge about the same. It's common practice to call your competitors to find the going rate and adjust yours accordingly. Some salons will go with what the traffic will bear.

What are the abilities of your stylists? Many accomplished stylists feel they are worth more and will refuse to work in value-priced salons. This is something to consider when you hire personnel or if you are considering the possibility of lowering or raising your price point.

Raise Your Prices

There will be a time when you will need to raise your prices. If you need to raise them in order to remain profitable, then do so. Most clients understand rising costs, but not of price gouging. You will lose clients and/or their trust if your increases are overly large and too far beyond those of your competitors. There will be times you may not be able to raise your prices, but find other creative ways of bringing more revenue into the salon. Here are some options: add extra services, add another product line, or seek an additional staff member with a clientele.

Secret: You may lose credibility if you raise them more than once a year.

A La Carte Pricing

Most salons have what we call *a la carte pricing;* all services are individually priced. Haircuts are priced according to the length of the hair. Shampoo, conditioners, blow-drying and styling are all extra, as well as cream rinses and color rinses. Permanents and color services cost extra. Many clients like the option of paying only for the service they need. They can omit the blow dry or styling if they so desire, then go home and style it themselves. It's a matter of personal preference.

A la carte is in contrast to packaged pricing. For example, you might pre-price two or three services together which cannot be separated, such as shampoo, haircut and blow style for $50.00 or more. Offer a shampoo, haircut, hair color, and a style for a charge of $175.00 as a package deal.

Create a Ticket of Services

Provide a pre-designed ticket of services to be given to each client by the receptionist. Each stylist signs the ticket with their name and checks off the service performed. Then the client returns the ticket to the receptionist for payment before they leave the salon. The stylist may also list recommended products.

If you are part of a franchise operation, you will not be able to set your own pricing. The franchiser will instruct you on when you can increase prices and by how much.

What to Charge Family and Friends

There is another important decision to make when setting prices. A rule must be set for how much to charge your friends and family for services they receive and products they purchase at your salon. You must also determine prices for your employees' friends and family. You can charge them all the same or make some distinction for your friends. I've heard of salon owners who choose to charge friends and family 50% of the total price, and pay wholesale for products.

Tip: I recommend that if you charge 50%, the money goes to the salon to cover expenses and the stylist forfeits their commission for the work on friends and family. Whatever you choose to do, make your employees aware of your policy when you hire them.

Sometimes stylists feel their services should be free to family whether they're doing a haircut or chemical processing. Setting firm boundaries from the beginning will prevent disputes later on.

Check Cashing Policies and Credit Cards

Another policy to think about from the beginning is how to receive money for your services. Some businesses want only cash, and others will allow checks and credit cards.

When you receive a check from a client, make sure that the date, address and phone number are current. Ask to see their driver's license and record the number on the back of the check. Produce three rubber stamps for your clients' checks. They can be made at your local printer or office supply store.

Use one to stamp the back of your clients checks. You will need blank spaces for their name, current address, phone number, social security number, place of employment, drivers license, and a credit card number. It will look like this:

Name: _____
Address: Phone: _____
Soc. Sec. No: # _____
Place of Employment: ____
Drivers License No: #_____
Credit Card No: #_____

Produce your second rubber stamp with the salon's name on it. It can be used on the front of your client's checks. It saves time for you and the customer, especially if your salon has a long name.

Have a third rubber stamp for endorsing the back portion of the checks you deposit. Use the following information:

For Deposit Only
Name of Your Salon
Name of Your Bank
Salon Checking Account Number

You have the right to ask for a driver's license if the client is paying by check and you don't know him/her. In fact, most clients expect to be asked for identification when writing checks. Of course you won't bother a regular client with this information because you will already have it on file. If the customer runs up a very large bill, you have the option of calling the client's bank for check approval. You may or may not want to accept out-of-town or out-of-state checks. Again, the option is yours. However, you will have no option if you own a salon in a tourist/resort area or a hotel salon where most clients are from abroad.

"Always follow up on bad checks. First, send a friendly reminder or make a phone call since accidents can happen."

The second notice could be a bit more firm. You have the right to take the bounced check to the bank and collect the money as soon as their account covers it.

You can use a small claims court to collect your money. Sometimes the client doesn't appear in court, then you don't get your money and you lose time away from work.

If you have a large number of problem checks, you can use a collection agency. They charge either a fee or take a portion of the money for collecting bad debts from clients. If the person moves, you probably won't ever get your money, so don't wait too long before you act.

It's amazing how many people write checks when they have no money, or worse yet, they write checks on closed accounts. So protect yourself, because it's a hassle, costly and time consuming to chase someone into court.

Most clients use debit or credit cards to make their purchases. It's good business to have a credit card machine. You'll lose sales if you don't have one. Statistics show that consumers who use charge cards tend to be more impulsive, and spend more money.

You'll pay a monthly fee, additional bank fees and a percentage on your sales. The bank will deduct that money monthly from your business checking account. Your best bet is to search around for a good deal. They will also make you sign a contract for a designated number of years. Credit card companies often approach you once you set up your DBA. They send a representative to the courthouse and search current records.

In Conclusion

Do your research before setting prices and try to be fair. See what the competition is charging and adjust your prices accordingly.

Notes:

CHAPTER FIFTEEN
Make it BIG with the Best Employees

Your human resources are the mainstay of your business. Make it really BIG by hiring employees who will support your efforts and want to be part of a winning team. Employees ultimately make or break your business. I suggest you choose them carefully. Many people asked me, "Where do you find such good employees?" I always appreciated the compliments and felt fortunate to have an excellent staff of well-trained, smart, dedicated and professional stylists. They were not only technically competent, but kind and good individuals.

Through my fourteen years as a salon employer, I attracted my employees in different ways. For the most part, licensed hair stylists were attracted to my salon through its good reputation. A busy location with a steady flow of new clients is always attractive to stylists looking to build a business. Everyone wants to be where the *money* is.

Attracting good stylists should be fairly easy if you have a nice, clean, reputable salon in a great location. Remember what I said about location, location, location? It's important on many levels. The stylists who are currently employed by you are a good indicator for available stylists. Talented stylists who have an outstanding reputation know and attract other professionals who want to work together.

I once met a stylist at a friend's social gathering. She applied a few weeks later, and I hired her. Her recommendation brought me another valuable employee. I found several employees through the classified section of the newspaper (pre-internet days). One of my best stylists was a co-worker from a neighborhood salon.

If you currently work in a salon, ask your co-workers if they would like to follow you. They may like you enough to work for you and they may also be ready for a change. When I left a salon to open my own business I asked one person to follow me and she did. A few years later, I ran into a former co-worker who asked me why I hadn't invited her too? I was speechless. My mistake was in thinking no one else wanted to leave. You won't know until you ask. There are many benefits to inviting current co-workers. It usually means more money in your pocket. They know you, are comfortable with you and probably like you. You most likely received similar training, which means you won't have to train them. They'll bring their clients and that means ... more money in your pocket.

Where to Find Potential Employees?

1. You can advertise in the classified ads of your local newspaper.

2. Cosmetology schools are a good source. There are thousands of cosmetology schools across the country. Many community colleges also have a program. Twenty five per cent of all trade schools in the U. S. teach beauty culture. Ask the school owner which students are ready to graduate. Set up an interview with each candidate.

I hired several young women right out of beauty school. Be prepared to spend extra time training them, or have them take advanced training at a qualified school of your choice.

3. Ask your friends if they know someone looking for a salon in which to work.

4. Sometimes unhappy stylists who want a salon change will seek out a new place. They hear of your new salon and want to join your team.

5. I've never been in favor of luring stylists away from competitive salons by offering more money or a higher commission, but it is done occasionally.

6. The internet is a good place to find employees. You can use job boards such as Career Builder, Monster.com, jobbuilder.com or CraigsList.org.

7. The E.D.D. or Unemployment Development Department in your area may have some leads for you.

How to Choose the Right Employees

When interviewing prospective employees, make them aware of the goals, purpose, and mission statement you developed during the planning stages of your salon. Explain in depth what you want to achieve, and pay attention to their responses. Perhaps you have a particular financial goal, or the goal of a spa or retail center. Maybe your purpose is to offer the most value for your services, or to offer your country location a real touch of class. Whatever it is, share it with them so they know they are expected to participate. When they know where you stand and what you expect from day one, potential employees can choose either to join your team for the right reasons or move on.

A good stylist can make money almost anywhere, but they won't find compatible goals or rewarding relationships in every salon. Teamwork isn't only about working together harmoniously and helping each other in the salon. It's also about sharing dreams, goals and ways in which to achieve them.

Secret: A prosperous clientele is not built up overnight. We all know it takes time to achieve a loyal following. Be sure your trainees and potential employees are aware that salon work is a long-term commitment.

Tip: You can download a free guide from the Intuit web site called "Hire your first Employee." http://www.intuit-hire.com/?cid=web_101

Eight Steps to the Hiring Process

Hiring good and lasting employees is a process that takes time and patience. Now more than ever salon owners must think through what they are looking for and search through resumes with a fine tooth comb. Employees either make or break your business, so it's important to choose those who are in some ways similar to you and in some ways different from you. This list should help you determine how to choose employees who will compliment you and your salon.

Step One: Determine *Your* Needs

Step one encourages you to determine what attributes, skills and experience are required to make your business a success for you, your employees, and the community. One of the most important things to keep in mind is how this individual will fit into the overall theme of your business. Will he or she fit the image you have developed for the salon? For example, if your clientele is youth oriented, then hire youthful stylists. A more sophisticated image will require stylists to dress and behave accordingly. You'll save yourself and the employee a lot of grief by choosing wisely.

Ask yourself some important questions:

1. Do you need certain skills in order to retain the type of clients you already have or plan to attract? If your clientele is largely male, then hire stylists who are adept at barbering or offer training to those who need barbering skills. Is this person technically competent?

2. Do you need self-motivated employees with these attributes: do superior work, listen intently, communicate intelligently with clients, and offer creative solutions?

3. Do you need employees who are willing to promote and sell salon products? Staff can be trained in sales skills. If your salon does not retail, then selling will not be a concern for you.

4. Do you need stylists who are well trained enough to support your salon's price point? Many salons have junior and senior stylists who receive a lower or higher pay according to their prior training and experience. Keep in mind that a stylist who earns less will have an incentive to work faster and smarter.

5. Does the prospective stylist fit in with the overall image you want to project to the public?

Exercise #1:

1. List salon functions and how many people you need for each function:

2. Describe the training employees need:

3. Define your compensation plan:

4. What employee characteristics do you want?

5. What is your image and what dress code will you enforce?

Exercise #2: Make up a job description for all employees so they are sure to understand the rules and what is expected of them. Have them sign it. Give each employee a copy for future reference.

- Stylist
- Haircutter
- Colorist
- Manicurist
- Salon coordinator or receptionist

Exercise #3: Write a Job Description

Job title: _____

Days/hours: _____

Job duties and responsibilities:

1. _____
2. _____
3. _____
4. _____
5. _____

Desired characteristics:

_____

Required qualifications of candidate: (specific skills, education, years of experience, license, etc.)

_____

_____

Commission/hourly wage, benefits, retail commission and other compensation:

Seek Useful Skills

Step Two encourages you to seek staff members who already have useful skills. Once you decide the specific skills you need from employees, choose from your applications and start the interview process. The following information is merely a suggestion list to refer to in case employee recruitment is a new experience for you.

1. The best candidates are smart, creative, enthusiastic, hard working, loyal and technically competent. They must be able to learn new techniques quickly.

2. Employees must maintain a clean and appropriate appearance. Salon policies define the dress code for all employees.

3. Another critical component is attitude. A positive attitude will carry a less experienced employee a long way. Many skills can be taught to an employee with an open mind and a positive *can do* mind set.

4. Your prospective employees must be able to work well with others. Most salons have a small staff working in close quarters. Team members must show initiative and cooperate by helping each other when necessary. It may be necessary to share clients when time is of the essence. This is the way to obtain optimal efficiency.

5. Stylists, manicurists, pedicurists, colorists, etc., must be punctual and stay on schedule. A client having more than one service will have a time schedule to follow according to the

appointment book and their own personal time limitations. Many clients resent being late for other appointments.

6. Stylists must use chemicals with care. Whoever performs chemical services must take the time and make the effort to follow instructions. Products vary, and do not always react like products used in the past or from another company. Many serious chemical mistakes occur by employees who do not read and follow directions.

7. Safety procedures are required for curling irons and blow dryers. These implements get incredibly hot, and can cause painful burns to the scalp and skin area.

8. Showing initiative is another necessary quality. The employee must be able to think on her/his feet. They must be ambitious and take the first step in making a client feel welcome: initiate the consultation, ask the client appropriate questions, be ready to suggest additional services, and sell suitable products. Each employee is responsible for the quality of work they produce. A good employee will keep their skills updated, learn product knowledge, support other team members, and show enthusiasm toward clients.

Another way that an employee can show initiative is to make suggestions when salon procedures need to be improved or updated. Giving feedback at salon meetings is crucial for improving the business.

9. Honesty is an area of concern when your employees handle money, have access to the supply room, or the keys to the salon. The salon owner/manager needs to simply pay attention and be

aware of anything out of the ordinary. My feeling on this is to always trust until you learn otherwise.

10. Products for the supply room and the back bar are expensive to stock. Teach your employees to be economical with the products. Show them how not to be wasteful, yet use the required products to get the best results.

11. Employees must develop good working habits by keeping their work area clean, and immediately clean their messes.

12. Reward employee dedication. It is always helpful when an employee is willing to work beyond business hours in case a client comes in at the last moment before closing. The salon is often a hectic environment and employees must be able to work well under pressure. Clients are sometimes overbooked, or there are miscommunications about appointment times. Unforeseen circumstances cause clients to be late or early, and ultimately miss their appointment time. Take note of stylists who have a dedication to their clients and the salon. Reward them from time to time.

13. Each employee must be a problem solver. Clients will make appointments, and may not know what they want or need. The employee must be able to do a consultation, make suggestions, and properly execute the service.

A client may arrive in the salon and needs a corrective procedure. Correcting chemical mistakes requires a lot of experience. Novice stylists may need to confer with the manufacturer or another more experienced colorist.

14. It is always recommended to hire healthy employees or those with a minimum of health problems. Salon life is hectic enough

without having a staff member who is constantly ill. It causes stress and chaos for the rest of the staff and clients.

15. Another potential issue is a staff member who takes time away from work to care for small children. Be sure to ask if the staff member has a dedicated baby sitter or other child care services. If not, you may have to cover for that person in the midst of your own busy schedule.

Application Form

Step Three is about knowing the person you are hiring on a deeper level. Develop your own application forms and photo-copy a supply of them. Ask questions that are most important to you. Included below is a list of questions I used in my salons:

Salon Application Form
Please print:

Name: _____ Date: _____

Address:

Phone number:

Social security number:

Beauty school attended:

How many years of salon experience?

Where did you previously work, for how long and reasons for leaving?

Why do you want to work here?

What salon services do you excel in?

What areas are you weak in?

Which products are you familiar with?

Do you feel comfortable selling products and services?

How do you feel about continuing education?

Do you have an existing clientele?

Do you prefer to work full time or part time?

Are you able to work early/late hours and weekends?

Will you help out with daily sanitation and other duties if requested?

Have you had any serious illness or injury? If so, explain.

Are you in agreement with the salons' policies regarding vacation, days' off and any benefits package?

Are you in agreement with the salon's goals, purpose, and mission statement?

If you were hired, what would you do to contribute to the overall success of this salon?

Do you have access to reliable transportation and a baby-sitter if necessary?

Have you ever been convicted of a felony?

Please give three references of people you have known for at least three years.

Name	Phone Number
_____	_____
_____	_____
_____	_____

Give me several good reasons why I should hire you.

Sign Name _____   Date _____

Prepare for the Interview

Step Four: Determine Employee Needs

In step four you discover what the employee wants out of the relationship. During your interview with potential employees, you need to find out what kind of situation the employee is looking for. Give yourself plenty of time for this. It is important not to rush the interview. Find a quiet place in the salon to do your interviews. Be patient and wait for them to think their answers through before speaking. Remember that potential employees are nervous, so make them feel comfortable to speak. Listen carefully and be objective in your analysis.

If the employee requires a baby-sitter or day care center, you could make suggestions for a reputable one nearby the salon.

192

Find the Secret to Motivating Employees

Step Five is about the constant task of motivating employees. Many salon owners complain that employees are not motivated. Attempting to motivate someone who doesn't care about your business and their relationship to it is a useless waste of time. Before hiring anyone discover their values and goals. The interview process will help you find what motivates the employee. You'll be able to use that information when you need it.

Ask about the employee's personal goals. For example, do they enjoy traveling, want to purchase a home or auto, get married, have children, or get a degree?

Ask about their vocational goals. What is their desirable weekly salary? How many days and hours do they want to work? Do they plan to open their own salon, and how soon? What are their problems?

When you are aware of what motivates them, you are better able to provide the means for their success. Align their goals to yours by building a bridge that joins your relationship for a higher purpose.

Tip: If you find that the employee has dreams of making big money, and your prices will not support their dream, then you would serve them and yourself better by suggesting an alternative place of employment. This is a time to be totally honest with the potential employee. If you cannot honestly serve their goals, you can be certain they will not participate in yours. They'll eventually leave and take your clients with them.

Meet with your employees regularly to monitor their goals. Motivate them to reach their goals, and be honest about what you believe is achievable in your salon.

Step Six: Implement the Employee Interview

Step six encourages an effective employee interview. Before the interview, show the candidate your written salon policies, mission statement, objectives, and goals. Ask their opinion, and listen carefully. Below is a list of probable questions. You may modify these or add questions that apply to your own situation. Your main objective here is to listen, listen, listen.

1. Ask what things in a salon setting are important to the employee?

2. What do they want from this salon that they didn't get from their previous places of employment?

3. Ask about their overall career objective.

4. Find out some of the things outside of their job that they have done or that they plan to do that will assist them in reaching their career objectives.

5. As a person, what do they feel they could most improve upon? As a stylist, what do they feel they could most improve upon?

6. Are there certain things they feel more confident in doing than others?

7. What are some of the things that motivate them?

8. What are their goals? Do they have clear goals that can be achieved? You should know what they are so you can assist in the attainment of the employee's goals.

9. Do they receive mental and emotional support from family and friends?

10. What do they have to offer the salon?

11. Ask how they could make your salon a better place to work?

12. Ask them to offer their insights on an appealing work environment.

13. What elements of this business do they enjoy?

14. What elements of this business excites them?

15. What elements of this business don't they like?

16. What would they change if they could, regarding past experiences.

Test Your Candidate

Step Seven asks you to test your employee candidate to determine their skill level. An employee with a well-known reputation may not need to be tested, but you have the right to see how each employee performs before hiring them. I applied at a salon that invited me to bring a model so the owner could see my work. It's also done in the restaurant industry. A potential candidate spends a few hours or a day working for free to show off their capabilities.

1. Have the prospective employee bring in a model to cut and style in front of you or your manager. Or you may supply the model.
2. Note how long the haircut takes, check accuracy, and watch the procedure. Neatness is important. Note the candidates' attitude with the model.
3. Ask the potential candidate to "sell" you a product or a service (as if you are the customer).

It is almost always trial and error when determining the talent of new employees. Sometimes you must trust your intuition. Most employers and employees understand there is a three month trial period. If the stylist does not work out you can dismiss the individual and start over, although training new people is time consuming. You may consider yourself lucky if your new candidate turns out to be technically competent with good working habits and a friendly personality.

A healthy employee is also a plus since it can be difficult to replace a stylist at a moments notice. The ill stylists' clientele will have to be switched to the other stylists who might already be busy.

Secret: There are three basic haircuts and every stylist must know how to cut: a layered cut, a wedge and a bob. All haircuts: past, present, and future will be a variation of these three cuts.

Tip: An important point for the salon owner and potential employee to remember is this: If there is no written contract stating the length of employment, then all employment is temporary. No matter how the interview goes, until the candidates prove themselves through their performance, the owner may terminate employment. Also, if the salon owner has misrepresented the salon to the potential employee, the employee has every right to terminate the employment situation at any time.

A probable test:
Use real or imagined situations that test a person's knowledge of the job. Begin with questions like "What would you do if" such and such happened? For instance, you could ask what would you do if you and another stylist were the only employees working in the salon on a particular day and the new stylist over-processed a client's permanent. Both stylist and client become upset with the results, and the stylist runs out of the salon crying, and leaves you alone to solve the problem. You are busy with your own clients. How would you handle this situation?

You could test candidates on any number of problematic situations that perhaps happened to you in the past. Good stylists must be problems-solvers, so it's a good idea to find out in the beginning how they would act or react in particular disturbing situations. What situation could you use to test your prospective employee?

Step Eight: Review and Choose

Step eight encourages you to review and choose your staff wisely. Interview several employees before making a hiring decision. Who to hire is often an intuitive process. Salon owners often choose potential employees who have a large clientele to bring with them. Before you make a hiring decision, be sure that this person is a team player, cooperative, and an asset to your salon. Otherwise your decision may backfire on you.

Many salons owners will not have the location, clientele, and prestige to offer an incredibly large paycheck. If a good employee is made aware that perhaps in time their goals will be attainable, they may be motivated to stay and build their clientele.

When it is obvious to you that the employee's goals are unattainable in your salon, then you might perhaps choose to pass that person up. They won't have staying power, and the situation could be frustrating for everyone involved. If you choose to keep the employee temporarily, then be aware that they may take clients with them when they leave.

Secret: It is a rule of thumb in this industry that employee/stylists turn over every three to five years. That was not my experience. A small percentage did come and go, but generally three fourths of my staff remained with me for an average of seven years.

Establish Goodwill

When an employee understands that you are willing to respect and honor who they are as a person and what they desire to achieve, they will generally offer you the same good will.

Establish a sense of family in your salon. Most salon staffs are small and employees quickly establish close relationships that sometimes exist apart from salon life. They often share professional and personal experiences and problems. The salon will benefit if these relationships remain harmonious.

Stylist Tools

Once a stylist or employee is hired, you must decide what tools they need to bring to your work place. This decision should be written in your policy section. All salons should furnish the products, unless there is a rental agreement, but opinions differ on what the stylists will bring to the salon as working tools. Some salons will furnish everything while others furnish nothing. The salon owner makes this decision.

Most stylists have all the necessary tools of the trade, especially if they recently graduated from beauty school. In my salon, I furnished all of the rollers, clips, perm rods, capes, towels, brushes, combs, and other tools.

Tip: I have always felt that shears, razors, clippers, irons, and blow dryers are personal items, and should be chosen and paid for by the stylist who uses them. These implements can be very costly to replace if not taken care of properly. You will also find, as I did, that the electrical appliances will not hit the floor as often if the stylist is the one who must replace them.

Employee Classifications

Instill an Anonymous System

Some salons, mainly the discount variety, have a system whereby they do not allow their stylists to use their real names or accept referrals. With this system each stylist is given a fictitious name and is rotated periodically. This practice prevents the stylist from gaining a following or taking their clients with them when they decide to move on to another salon or go into business for themselves. Any new stylist will automatically fit in where the last one left off and will gain a full clientele. This system is ideal for a salon that wants to build salon loyalty rather than stylist loyalty. This procedure is advantageous for a new stylist who doesn't like to wait around for a year or so to develop his or her own clientele. Nothing is more discouraging to a new stylist than sitting around for long periods of time waiting for clients to walk in.

The disadvantage of this system is that the client cannot request a favorite stylist and many people don't like that. Clients become comfortable with the stylist's personality. The argument for this system is that theoretically all stylists are trained to cut hair the same, which, if possible, could have its advantages. You must then ask yourself if you are hiring a machine or a creative individual?

During one of my early years as a stylist, I attended a trade show in Chicago. One of the platform artists said to the audience of hairdressers "Don't tell me how good you are, tell me how much money you make?" According to this educator, a stylist's skills are important, yet equally important is the ability to utilize those skills to the benefit of the client. Satisfaction is what keeps clients coming back for more.

The Scoop on Independent Contractors

Some employers hire people to work for them as independent contractors. As the business owner you aren't required to withhold taxes. You don't have to pay Workman's Compensation premiums, unemployment taxes and matching social security taxes (FICA). Nor do you have to provide fringe benefits such as health insurance, paid vacations, sick leave and retirement plans. If you pay an independent contractor $600.00 or more during the year, you must file a form 1099-MISC.

The IRS has determined a list of factors to determine if a person has the status of employee or independent contractor. The degree of importance of each factor varies according to the profession and the conditions in which the services are performed. The most important factor is employer control. If the business owner has the right to control how and when a person works, then that person is most likely to be considered an employee. The key elements in contract work involves these factors: who regulates the type of work and how, where and when it's done, who determines the fee structure, who receives the money from clients, who provides the equipment and supplies, and who generates the clientele.

The two best ways to minimize the risk of your independent contractor being reclassified as an employee is to make certain that this person has multiple sources of income. Be careful how you classify these people. Just because you call them an independent contractor doesn't make it so. If in doubt speak with your accountant or attorney or have the IRS determine whether a worker is an employee by filing form SS-8.

The downside to this is that if the IRS determines that your independent contractors are or were indeed employees, you may be required to pay fines of up to 100% of the tax. The fine percentage may change, so you may want to refer to your accountant for updates.

Hire a Salon Coordinator, Receptionist, or Manager

The salon coordinator, receptionist or manager is a valuable staff member in the salon. I am using three different titles for this position, but generally in a small salon one person will fill all three positions. A very large salon may have up to three different people who fill these positions. If the owner is a stylist/manager, then he or she will invariably hire a receptionist to manage the desk and all its duties. An absentee owner will generally hire a manager or receptionist to handle daily business operations.

There are five main responsibilities of the small business owner or manager. They must recruit, select, train, motivate, and manage employees. Motivation and management should be virtually effortless when you recruit and select employees who are technically competent and in agreement with your purpose, mission statement and goals.

The manager will wear many hats. The duties include: opening and closing the salon, setting it up for business, handling checks, credit cards and cash, coordinating the desk and appointments, purchasing supplies, meeting with salespeople, and implementing the marketing plan.

The general title for anyone who does the overall managing of the salon is called the Salon Coordinator, so to prevent confusion we will use that title throughout this chapter.

Management Qualifications

What are the qualifications needed to run the business part of your salon? List qualities which you believe are important, then read the information below. You can adjust your responses accordingly.

The salon coordinator sets the pace for the entire salon. He/she may be the first encounter the potential client has with your business. This person establishes the image and philosophy of your business. It is essential to have the right person with the proper skills. Take the time to define this job description as accurately as possible. You will then be able to interview and choose the best candidate for the job.

1. Determine whether the position will be full-time or part-time.

2. What hours will you require that person to work?

3. Extended hours may require more than one manager.

Establish the pay rate according to the demands of the position and the skill level required.

When designing the questions for your interview, keep in mind the salon's distinct personality. You will want a salon coordinator who harmonizes with the salon and its staff. Once you have interviewed and chosen a coordinator, you must then train them in your particular manner of doing business.

It is best if they have previous experience. A potential coordinator who has a solid background with experience in different types of salon atmospheres and in handling a variety of clients will certainly be an asset to your business. You must then be supportive of this person, and give them a sense of family and teamwork.

Trick: It is important to trust your salon coordinator/manager to be an authority figure and not present conflicts with their decision making process. Have an implicit trust in his/her ability to handle all affairs.

Three Critical Characteristics of the Salon Coordinator

1. First of all, the coordinator must have unlimited patience, be personable, well-groomed, friendly, exude authority, a friendly voice and a helpful manner. The coordinator should call clients by name. The appointment book will give a listing. They must be caring, and sensitive to your clients needs. A smile and a compliment goes a long way.

2. The coordinator should also be able to distance his or herself from the staff, especially if you require him or her to be your manager. It's very difficult for some people to manage close friends. Often the friends don't understand that the relationship must change in order for the manager to be more effective. If issues arise regarding job performance, they need to be handled diplomatically and quickly.

3. Salon coordinators must be open to concerns of the staff. They often have creative, imaginative, and efficient methods of conducting their work. They may have some surprising abilities that when allowed to come forth, will be an asset to your business. Give your staff the authority to make decisions. Make certain they understand your policies and know when to take the proper action.

Tip. Remember that constantly monitoring your staff (micro-managing) and over-controlling are a sure way to suffocate team spirit and the growth of your business.

Responsibilities of the Salon Coordinator

The salon coordinators' duties may be some or all of the following:

- Answer the telephone in a professional and cordial manner. Identify who they are to the client and ask how they can be of service. Make appointments with the requested employee. Request the client's phone number in case you need to verify or change the appointment. Repeat the clients' name, service, date, and time back to the client for approval. You could develop your own precise script for telephone answering procedures.

- Greet all new clients as they enter the salon, introduce yourself to them, introduce them to their stylist, and reassure them of your staff's abilities. Offer clients a beverage, styling books, or the changing room.

- Accept any cash and attain information for the back of checks or credit cards.

- Learn how to write sales receipts.

- Make appointments for the stylists. The salon coordinator should have knowledge of the various services and how much time they require. Booking appointments must be done with care. Services are sold in terms of time on the appointment page or computer, which may spell either a gain or a loss. The appointment book divides the stylists working time to suit the clients' service. This book should reflect what services are taking place at any given time. Higher profits for the salon and a good salary for the stylist are the rewards for fast work and effective scheduling.

- **Tip:** I recommend that the salon coordinator call clients who are receiving a chemical service for the first time. This will serve as a reminder to the client and cut out lost time for no-shows. You may find it advantageous to get phone numbers for all call-ins, not just for clients receiving high-priced tickets. And of course if you send birthday greetings, newsletters, enewsletters and direct mail, you will also want addresses and email addresses as well.

- Service records for services performed and merchandise sold should be retained for every client. These records belong to the salon, not to the individual stylist. They should be returned to the salon file or entered into the computer program after use.

Retain the following:

Name and address of client
Phone number
Date of service or purchase
Service rendered and price
Product used, along with results and any notes
Name of stylist who performed the service

- Take inventory: order, price and stock supplies. The salon coordinator maintains a good working relationship with the distributor salespeople or any other sales representatives who supply the salon.

- Be a salesperson for the salon by answering questions about products and services and making recommendations or substitutions.

- The salon coordinator keeps accurate records by doing a certain amount of daily and weekly bookkeeping. She'll account for commissions from services and products, incidental expenditures from the cash register or payment drawer, and keep track of receipts.

- Keep reception and salon areas clean and orderly. Dust, organize and price retail products.

- One of the most helpful duties a coordinator performs is to distribute new clients in a fair manner. Many arguments and jealousies erupt from the stylist who always runs to the phone or door first to snatch up the walk-in clients. Nothing can destroy team spirit quicker than a selfish stylist. If you can't find or afford a good coordinator, develop a policy for distributing new clients in a fair manner. Insist that each stylist follow the rules or they will be dismissed.

- Generally the new client will go to the stylist who is not busy at the time the client walks in. Some salons have a policy where the first stylist who arrives in the morning receives the first walk-in (provided they aren't busy already). The second stylist to arrive gets the second client and so on. You could also go by seniority or draw numbers. Another solution to this problem is to put all employees on a fixed or hourly salary.

- The salon coordinator will also be taking phone messages for all employees. Information must be logged as to who called, their phone number, when the call was made and when it can be returned. Emergency messages need to be relayed as soon as possible.

- If your salon has a computer, the coordinator would tally up all receipts at the end of the day.

- A salon providing computer imaging must also keep track of client consultations.

- Define the procedures for closing the business at the end of the day. Whoever opens and closes the salon is the only employee who needs access to the keys. Otherwise it is impossible to monitor salon hours and activity.

One evening I drove past my salon and noticed the lights were on. It was late and we closed hours before. I went in to investigate and an employee was giving her two friends free chemical services, using my products, electricity and water. It was a disturbing situation. This is a good reason to not freely pass out keys to your staff.

The Advantages of Hiring a Shampoo Attendant

Shampoo attendants can be utilized to supplement and compliment your staff. Clients consider a salon with a shampoo attendant to be more prestigious. The benefits are that these employees will shampoo and condition clients more thoroughly than a stylist who is in a hurry. They save time by servicing clients who are in a hurry or are uncomfortable with sitting and waiting for the stylist. This procedure gives the stylist added time to spend with cutting, styling, perming, or just catching up with their appointments. Shampoo attendants can also save time and make more money for the salon by helping with time consuming services. They can assist the stylist with chemical services by processing, rinsing and unwrapping perms, and by rinsing, shampooing, and conditioning a hair color client. This employee generally prepares the client for the skilled functions of the stylist.

The shampoo attendant's duties may also include:
1. Refill and stock supplies at the back bar.
2. Laundering and folding towels.
3. Educate the client regarding shampoos and conditioning treatments.

Shampooing can be a tough backbreaking job, so your shampoo attendant will need periodic rest periods. Some clients will also tip the shampoo attendant for the extra service.

Make it BIG With a Manicurist or Nail Technician

You can make a BIG income with a manicurist or nail technician. You may even consider adding on a new nail salon. Nail services have become increasingly popular. Articulate career women have grown to be more conscious of their total appearance and include nail services to their weekly or monthly beauty regimen. The application of artificial nails as a salon service has been a booming success and will continue as more women join the work force and acquire more disposable income. With development of new products and techniques, nail services are an integral part of the salon menu. The nature of this service demands a repeat visit to the technician for re-application. Greater revenues are generated due to repeat visits.

Nail care offers an attractive profit margin with minimum expenditure. Technicians require a quality table, a comfortable chair or stool on wheels, a lamp, and a complete line of supplies. Speak to your distributor salesperson about the overall cost of setting up a nail center.

Actual floor space needed is minimal, creating a high square-footage profitability area. Retail sales also benefit from this type of service, so be sure to stock the most popular nail care products. Clients are ready to purchase whatever the nail expert recommends to maintain their nails at home.

Manufacturers are working to perfect products and tools such as odorless acrylic formulas, emery boards which create fewer filings and longer lasting chip resistant enamels.

Nail grooming centers are not only indigenous to hair salons, but are equally as popular in shopping malls and busy commercial areas as independently owned *stand alone* nail centers. These nail centers offer manicures, a variety of artificial nails, and pedicures. One local nail center also sells retail items to their female clients: purses, scarves, hats, jewelry and other attractive items.

Manicurists and nail technicians generally receive a commission compensation; 50% is the average, plus 10-15% of retail products sold. You could also offer a salary instead.

Make it BIG With an Esthetician

There are BIG profits in cosmetics and skin care services. An esthetician is a skin care professional who is trained in cosmetic skin care treatments including facials, hair removal (waxing and threading), massage, body wraps, eyebrow tinting, make up application and permanent makeup. The esthetician may also be trained in electrolysis – permanent hair removal. They typically work in salons or day spas and need an esthetician license.

Some cosmetologists take an interest in skin care and get extra training in order to offer facials, waxing, massage and make up application. It's advantageous to have a private room for skin care services away from the noise and bustle of the salon.

Cleaning Service or Attendants

Keeping a clean salon is not just a suggestion but is mandatory from the perspective of the state board, and for the public as well. No one wants their appearance to be maintained in a dirty salon. It is imperative that the salon be kept neat and sanitized.

If you don't have the time or energy to do it yourself, then get estimates from local cleaning businesses. Have them come in once a week for a thorough cleaning, although the salon will need a surface cleaning almost daily. You can arrange periodic visits from a carpet and floor cleaning service too.

Employee Compensation

There are several ways in which to compensate your employees. A commission basis is the most traditional way. Fifty percent for the stylist and fifty percent for the salon is the norm, however, variations exist. You may offer an inexperienced stylist less, such as forty to forty five percent then increase the percentage as the stylist gains experience and clients.

Some salons pay according to a stylists' referral rate. As referrals increase, so does the stylists' salary or commission. You can offer a candidate with a large following a higher percentage, such as fifty five or sixty percent in order to attract the stylist to your salon. You may be generous to offer a higher commission, but always be aware of your bottom line. Too high of commissions eat into profit potential.

Another option that is gaining in popularity is salary compensation. Each stylist is paid a salary according to that person's ability and overall contribution to the salon. Cost-average the stylists' last six months of revenue, and find an amount agreeable to both parties. It is important to review the salary compensation every four to six months as the stylists' client list either grows or declines in volume. Unless you are paying every stylist the same, it would be necessary to keep individual compensations a private matter. At this point, you may consider writing a contract in order to define the details of the transaction.

Stylists' are generally paid a 10% commission on the retail products they sell. They certainly deserve a compensation for their time and effort in educating themselves and clients about the products. You can pay a higher commission if you so desire, but your average mark-up is generally about 30-50%. Remember that it is your money (products) sitting on the shelves. You are spending valuable time to choose it, order it, count it, price it, stock it, store it, dust it, and watch after it. Compensate yourself first.

You will be required by the federal government to pay taxes on all retail commissions. Pay your stylists' retail commissions often: every two weeks or once a month. Let them see that retailing really is worth the effort, and they need not be afraid of rejection. I posted monthly retail profits in the employee lounge. The stylists could then compare their earnings. After a while I discovered they were consciously competing for the number one spot, and the year-end bonus for highest retail commissions.

Motivate Your Way to Success

Motivational Tools for Your Salon
Motivating employees can be a major problem for many salon owners, managers and employees. There are many different ways in which to do this.

Avoid the Challenge of Motivating Employees:

1. Establish your goals and purpose
Share it with employees, and express how your goals and

theirs will create a win-win situation. Chunk down your goals so every quarter there is something to aim for.

2. Share your position in the community
Let the employee understand your commitment to the community and explain how they can help you by attending networking events and passing out cards to local inhabitants.

3. Respect the employee's goals
You learned of their goals, and periodically review your documentation. Mention their goals whenever you find them faltering in their work. Use their goals to motivate them to be more productive.

4. Be a good role model
You must be a good role model and continually contribute to and personally exhibit a motivated attitude. When your upbeat attitude is authentic and sincere, it will spread and increase on a daily basis.

5. Give encouragement
Help employees who are not doing as well financially as others. They may need additional training. Employees may become disenchanted if they are not reaching their goals. Think of ways to keep them from becoming bored and frustrated.

6. Provide audio, videotape/DVD training
An excellent way in which to boost morale is to purchase audio and video tapes/DVD specifically made to enhance employee attitude. They can be loaned to employees for listening at their convenience. If you have a television and a DVD player, your group can learn together during a staff meeting.

Invite employees to your home as a social event, view the information and discuss possibilities in a more relaxed environment. There are many good books available at cosmetology conferences, through trade magazines, and through your distributor salesperson.

7. Attend trade shows or hire live trainers

Many trade shows will present at least one motivational speaker whose entire speech is geared toward cosmetologists. Your group could attend the event together, and later discuss what they learned and how they could personally improve performance and attitude. Sometimes you can find a local motivational speaker who will come into your salon for an hour or so and speak with your employees.

8. Employee benefits as a motivational tool

You are not obligated to offer benefits, although benefits are a good incentive to attract and keep good employees. Don't forget, you are competing with other service industries for employees such as food service, office, sales, health care, hospitality, and other career options.

Few salons offer incentives such as paid vacation and health insurance. If you find health benefits too expensive, you can pay a portion of it and have the employees make up the balance. You can also use a portion of the stylist's commission from retail sales to subsidize a health insurance plan.

Other benefits can include free or partially paid tickets to educational events, lunches or dinners at such events, or a paid hotel room for overnight stays. Birthday and holiday gifts are also extra-added bonuses.

You may also offer a bonus to the stylist with the highest retail sales, the most permanent wave or color services or the most client referrals. Recognition and bonuses should be in direct relation with how much each stylist contributes to the overall success of the salon.

9. Social events as a motivator

Remember that employees in other occupations are given benefits and perks. You may or may not have a medical plan or paid vacation, but you can offer other benefits which add to a sense of camaraderie in your salon.

A Christmas party or dinner for your employees in a nice restaurant, an elegant setting, or the comfort of your home would be an appreciative gesture. One year I picked up each of my employees at their home in a limousine and took them to an elegant Christmas brunch. Have a Halloween party at the salon where all employees dress in costume. It's a fun way in which to creatively express themselves and entertain your clients. A summer picnic in a local park or at a nearby beach can be another casual way of saying *thank-you* to your employees and their families. Provide food, beverages, games, and prizes or perhaps small gifts for the children.

Remember your employees' birthday with a card, and a present or gift certificate or flowers.

10. Reward systems as a motivator

There are many ways to reward employees for their loyalty and good work. A year end bonus is a good way of retaining, motivating, and thanking employees whose overall performance has contributed to the success of your salon.

Contests are another way to motivate staff and increase salon income. Contests could be monthly, quarterly, or yearly. You could give a cash prize for the employee who sells the most retail products, attracts the most new clients, sells additional chemical services over their average, gets the most referrals, etc.

Recognize employees who offer speaking engagements or enter cutting and styling contests to promote their creativity.

I once promoted *the salon profession* at Career Day at our local high school. I spoke of salon life to curious students.

Newspaper exposure with a photograph is always a nice reward for an employee who goes the extra mile. It shows that you are appreciative of their efforts and recognize their talent.

11. Staff meetings as a motivator

Staff meetings are an excellent time to establish a sense of team-work. Good working relationships are important in the salon. Meetings can take place in the salon after hours. Mix business and pleasure by having your meeting in a quiet restaurant where everyone feels more relaxed and is away from the bustling salon atmosphere. Meeting in a semi-social situation is a good way for employees to enjoy each other's company without interruptions.

Staff meetings should be a regular occurrence in every salon. Meetings may take place once a month or so, depending on urgency.

Don't let the discussion turn into a gripe session. The owner or manager should set goals and choose the topics of conversation.

Motivation, new styles, new products and techniques can be discussed. There's nothing worse than to have a new product on the shelf that no one knows about or what it does. It's particularly embarrassing when a client notices it first.

You can also ask a company representative to conduct an in-salon educational class on new products. If you have the resources, you can schedule a motivational speaker or a sales training expert to talk to your staff.

Some salon owners establish goals, and salon procedures on their own; others include the staff in making important decisions that affect everyone. During staff meetings you can discuss goals and objectives; and brainstorm ideas for the coming year. This is also a time to review policies and business procedures. You may discuss ways in which to make the business better; suggest new promotional ideas, assess which promotions didn't work, and what contributions were made by employees other than the usual day to day routine.

Tip: Staff meetings are a good time to compliment your staff on their performances.

12. Continuing education as a motivational tool

The cosmetology industry is constantly changing. I cannot stress enough the importance of continuing education. This pertains not only to stylists who must learn about new products and techniques, but to salon owners and managers as well.

To be competitive, it is critical to know in advance which products and which styles will be popular in order to meet consumer demand. Attend trade shows to learn about new products and styles. Read trade and fashion magazines to find out current trends. Pay attention to the hairstyles of trendsetters: celebrities, pop stars, television and movie actresses and actors.

Management training seminars offer assistance to managers who may have problems dealing with or motivating employees. Managers can be trained to make decisions more effectively.

Trade magazines, promotional flyers and your distributor salesperson offer up to date information about educational events for stylists, manicurists, estheticians and managers.

13. In-salon training

Many salons have their own training program. A staff member or team of staff members train new stylists to cut, style, color, and perm using their own unique system. In this case, the salon trains all new employees to perform the same. Stylists are generally paid minimum wage for a forty hour week during this assistant-ship training. They may also be required to sign a contract to stay for 6 months or a year (whatever duration is required) so you get a return on your educational investment.

Many salons do not have the time, space, or energy to train novice employees. National and International trade shows generally offer hands-on educational events specifically designed to educate stylists on new cuts, styles and techniques. A

216

reputable advanced training school is a good place to learn the newest techniques and procedures. Periodic training in motivation and client retention will aid in keeping stylists and clients happy.

A new stylist could be trained first as an assistant to one or several senior stylists. They would spend a certain amount of time learning their trade one on one from the senior stylist. Eventually they acquire a chair when their skills are upgraded.

Computer training is important for all employees. If you choose to implement a computer, be patient and give employees time to absorb the information. Assure them that it is easy to use and will allow them to quickly track their efficiency.

14. Let go of deadbeats

I'm sorry to say that every once in a while you run across a deadbeat employee. They complain about everything ... including you. They have control issues, their life is a mess, and no one can do anything to their satisfaction. You must always be aware when a deadbeat employee is beginning to sabotage your salon spirit. One angry or frustrated employee can bring about a negative environment causing hostility and resentment for everyone. They are just plain unhappy, and no amount of motivation will help them.

Promote positive thinking by meeting with that person directly to discover how the problem can be resolved. If you can't come to a peaceful resolution, your only recourse is to let that person go to find happiness elsewhere.

Win BIG with Trade Shows

Trade shows are excellent as a motivating tool for your staff. They provide the education, excitement, and glamour in the cosmetology profession and motivate you to look, perform, and be your very best.

For a relatively small price, you are able to attend workshops and events taught by the industry's most renown celebrities: artistic teachers, progressive leaders, motivational speakers, and foremost salespeople. Either by observation or hands on experience, you'll learn the newest and trendiest cuts, styles, color systems, and permanent wave techniques. Hands-on classes are generally at an additional price, but much more effective than the observation method of learning.

There is also additional education in aesthetics and nail treatments. You can learn all about hair removal methods like hair waxing, and at the opposite end of the spectrum you can purchase hairpieces and hair extensions.

There will also be the opportunity to investigate salon styling books, fashion magazines, educational videos, computer imaging systems, computer bookkeeping systems, and motivational audio CD's and DVD's. You can *oooh* and *aaah* over the newest in salon equipment: reception room seating, desks and showcases, stylist workstations, back bar systems, manicure tables, facial equipment, and roller carts to all dimensions of salon tools. You will find a vast array of styling shears, clippers, blow dryers, curling irons, combs, brushes, capes, drapes, aprons and much more.

And then there are the fun non-essentials for the stylist like manufacturer inspired tee-shirts, sweatshirts, caps, watches, jewelry, handbags, coffee cups and more.

You will be exposed to a staggering amount of potential retail items like hair decorations, jewelry, sequined clothes, cosmetic bags, and even toys. Most of the products found at the show can be resold at retail prices in the salon, while some are reserved for professional salon use only.

Trade shows have become more commercial in the last thirty years. They will lure you with the glitz and glamour of high tech video clips, choreographed dance productions, exotic models, and sassy music. The artists effectively project a mixed image of excitement, sensuality, and professionalism.

Many of the major manufacturers have become product oriented and will provide you with an immense amount of their personal logo products to take home or back to the salon. Having promotional paraphernalia sitting around demonstrates to the client how much you support the products you use.

Whichever way you look at it, trade shows are a wonderful way to get out of town for the weekend, rub elbows with other salon owners and employees, have fun, shop for goodies, get a top notch education, and last but not least get motivated to go back to your salon and make a difference.

Trade Magazines for the Inside Scoop

Trade magazines are important publications to keep you abreast of any trends, new products, techniques, equipment, and any changes in the cosmetology industry. These magazines are informative and should be read by the salon owner, manager, and stylists alike. They are to be kept in the employee lounge, away from the clients' magazines. Clients have no business looking at trade magazines or professional literature.

Create your own personalized scrapbook of favorite photos. They can be clipped from current haircut and hairstyle books and magazines or from your own photographs. Add your own quotes of information on what is popular and is easy care. Suggest perming and coloring possibilities or alternative styling tips.

Keep a record of your subscriptions: name of magazines, when you subscribed, length of subscription and cost. All trade and leisure publications, and client styling books are tax deductible.

Get Value From Your Salon Dress Code

When I started in the cosmetology profession back in the 1960's, stylists were known as beauticians or beauty operators, and we were required to wear plain white polyester uniforms and thick rubber-soled white shoes. That particular look was considered professional salon attire. The uniform is still required in beauty school, but not in a professional salon.

As a salon owner, you have the right to decide which fashions are suitable for your style of salon and the image you want to project to the public. State your position on fashion and image when hiring employees so they fully comprehend where you stand on the issue. By all means, when someone slips, you must quickly reinforce your stance.

The clothes your employees wear should reflect the decorum of your business. For example, blue jeans and sneakers would not look appropriate in a prestigious elegantly decorated salon. One rule that always works for the salon owner, receptionist and employees is to *dress for success.* If that means a tie and sport jacket for the men stylists, then so be it. If it means dressing up in casual elegant fashions or business attire for the women, then that is what they must wear.

"The *rule of thumb* is this: always remember who your customers are and the impression you want to make."

Today a professional looking hairstylist can be dressed in anything from casual sportswear to stylish dresses. High heels can be worn, but ouch!

Fad styles or business attire are appropriate in some situations. Some salon owners ask their employees to wear matching smocks or aprons.

If there is a problem with keeping a dress code, you might ask all employees to wear black and white coordinates. It always looks clean, crisp, and fresh. This takes dressing out of the hands of stylists who don't want to or know how to dress in a professional manner. Employees who want to be considered a pro and be paid like a pro need to dress for the part.

Again, the rule of thumb is to always sell your salon image. Maybe a grunge look is required: torn jeans, worn out boots or gym shoes and general grunge wear. Make an alternative statement by hiring stylists who wear dread locks or a combination of multi-colored hair, or half shaved heads and body piercing. There is certainly a market for the grunge look. There are salons for neighborhood kids who engage in the punk or rap scene. Represent them in fashion and in attitude and they are yours.

Exercise: What dress code will you implement?

Educate Your Staff about Products

Educate your staff on how to use your products. Doing so will save you money and help control your bottom line. Wasting product is a major concern of most salon owners. How can you control wastefulness? One solution is to monitor your buying habits and by making smart purchasing decisions. The conservative owner can *buy smart* by purchasing their products in bulk or through special sales from distributors.

Make every effort to teach your employees to be conservative with professional products. Teach them not to use less than what they need, nor more than what they should in order to achieve the desired results. Expensive shampoos and conditioners needlessly going down the drain will soon drain your bottom line. A conscious shampoo attendant can minimize waste at the shampoo bar.

Tip: Ask your stylists or color technicians not to pre-mix tints and bleaches. Wait until the client has arrived and is seated in the salon. If the client doesn't show up or changes their mind about having a color treatment, then the pre-mixed product isn't wasted.

In Conclusion

Your human resources are your most valuable commodity. You know you can't do this alone. You need the support of a competent, smart, caring and assertive staff. Choose them wisely to get your winning team.

Notes:

CHAPTER SIXTEEN
Maximize Salon Potential

Every salon, no matter how it starts out, has the potential to become your dream come true. With a good work ethic you can make that *beauty shop on a shoestring* into your perfect dream business.

Add impact to your goals by finding a balance between minimizing risk and maximizing your potential. There are potential risks in any business endeavor, and they can be minimized through education, patience, and communication.

Super Solutions

A large part of business ownership is problem solving. A smart entrepreneur will solve problems in an efficient, systematic and professional manner. Study the people who excel in management techniques and follow their lead. Will you make mistakes? Probably. We've all heard the expression "experience is the best teacher." Do your best to be fair and just with everyone. Learn from your mistakes and move on. Remember the mistakes of salon owners you worked for and make a list or a mental note of what *not* to do. That will put you ahead of the game.

Learning relaxation techniques and letting go of minor disturbances will help you to develop more patience. Learn not to react, but to step back for a few moments and think through your next steps.

Do yourself a big favor and learn good communication skills

by creating a two-way understanding. Be open to what others have to say. Spend more time listening than speaking. Create a win-win situation for everyone involved.

When you know in advance what leads to misunderstandings you will most likely avoid troubled situations or prevent them before they get out of control. Immediately address the problem and find the most creative and benevolent solution.

How to Keep Your Clients

Before we can discuss how to keep your clients, we need to find out what makes them leave. According to marketing statistics: 1% die, 3% move away, 5% develop other relationships, 9% go to the competition, 14% are dissatisfied with their product or service, and the largest majority of customers, 68%, leave because they were upset with their treatment.

Clients are often dissatisfied and upset because of poor customer service. Here we have a list of nine consumer complaints:

1. Poor training of employees.
2. No business philosophy.
3. Employees who don't care.
4. Perceptual differences of what they want or need.
5. Perceptual differences of what is provided and what is received.
6. Negative attitude of employees.
7. Improper handling of complaints.
8. No company set of standards.
9. Employees not given authority to make decisions.

This list of consumer complaints vividly discloses the problem with small business today. It is apparent that your human resources are your most precious commodities. Your employees must have the necessary skills, be well trained, and be courteous to your customers.

So the question becomes "How can we improve our competency, our listening skills, and customer service?" The number one thing we all want is customer loyalty. We want that client to return over and over throughout the years. How do we do that? Improve competency by staying abreast of current trends. Attend trade shows and make suggestions to clients who are bored with their appearance. Listen to what the client is saying to you. Do your best to comply. Good customer service is about paying attention to the client's needs or desires. If you can't please that person, step away and allow someone else to take over. It's better to keep the client in-house rather than go to the competition.

In *Chapter One: The BIGGEST Secret of All*, I stated, "It's all about the client" and it's as true now as it was then. Remember too that the buck stops with you. It all goes back to you, and your ability to choose and train people who represent your business well and reflect your philosophy.

Here is a list of fourteen guidelines to help you realize a successful and fulfilling business experience.

Ensure Salon Success: Fourteen Guidelines

1. Review the Whole Picture
Once the decision has been made to start a business, many salon owners become enthusiastic about the venture and get caught up in the daily routine. Periodically step back and review the whole picture. Be certain that all problems have been addressed and your goals are being met on some level. As owners, we tend to concentrate on the technical rather than the strategic work at hand. At a trade conference many years ago, one professional

speaker said (of salon owner's business skills), "Ninety percent of salon owners are in a coma." Entrepreneurs are too concerned with working on *my* business as opposed to working *in* the business. Step back and open your eyes!

2. Learn How to Plan

The two major reasons most businesses fail are due to *mismanagement* and *under capitalization*. Mismanagement is generally the result of poor planning. Without a viable business plan, an entrepreneur is apt to run their business haphazardly. No road map, no destination. The days of *winging it* are over. Develop a business plan.

3. Evaluate Your Strengths and Weaknesses

A good business manager needs to evaluate their strengths and weaknesses. Talk to friends, partners, and family about what they honestly perceive to be your strengths and weaknesses. You might be surprised at what you hear. Be realistic with what you are good at, and where you need coaching or education.

Get advice when you need it. The cost of an hour or so with an attorney, accountant or marketing person can save you a great deal of money and aggravation in the long run.

4. Research the Marketplace

Business people don't have to be psychics, but they must be able to anticipate obstacles. Is a new shopping center opening near your business? Call management and find out if a new salon is moving into your mall. You may have to rethink your plans, or prepare for some drastic changes due to new competition.

5. Plan Your Financial Resources

Proper budgeting is important. Know where your money is going. Slim down costs on unnecessary expenses to allow for increased rent, supplies, or needed promotions. Keep your bookkeeping accurate, save your receipts and watch where your petty cash is going. Think economically by purchasing some items in bulk amounts.

Under capitalization can be a major problem for small business owners. Project your start up costs so you have enough money until you are established. Learn to build equity in your business. Your business may need to be firmly established before you are able to draw a salary. Plan this as part of your budget if it applies to your situation.

Tip: Create a comfortable cushion for your personal life before you begin. It is counterproductive to withdraw needed money from your business to maintain your household.

6. Upgrade Your Skills

People are not born with business skills. You may have a good business sense, but there's no substitute for tried and true knowledge. Here are some suggestions:

    A. Take a small business management class.

    B. Read business books that give comprehensive guidelines for success.

    C. Subscribe to entrepreneurial magazines. Look for salon management magazines.

    D. There are lots of free marketing classes on the internet.

7. Find a Mentor

Find a mentor who knows the ropes. They can give you valuable advice and touch on solutions you would never think of. You'll be glad you did.

8. Learn How to Trade Services

Be creative in obtaining what you need. Be willing to trade services if possible. Take the initiative and call advertisers, construction people etc., to see if they might be interested in a trade. You will be more effective if you speak face to face with them. Let your creativity, talent, and persistence be the qualities that will balance out the shortage of start-up resources.

9. Be Practical

Instead of going to a lawyer when business situations appear to be overwhelming, try a therapist or consultant first.

10. Train Yourself First

In the cosmetology industry we tend to be overly dependent on employees. We hire employees who specialize in areas we know little about or have no time to learn. The correct method is for the entrepreneur to learn the process first, then train employees on how it should be done in his or her salon.

11. Develop a Marketing Strategy

Another reason for salon failure is that there is no marketing strategy for success. We need to know who our customers are. Important factors such as customer age, geographic location, and family size can have an impact on what and how they buy.

12. Know Your Market

Lack of market knowledge is a major problem. Know what your competition is doing and make every attempt to do it better.

13. Develop Quality Control

One problem with small businesses is an absence of a standardized quality control program. Attaining better results and better serving your clients are your number one priorities. Send out surveys, and ask for feedback from your clients on the quality of your services.

14. Re-Energize Yourself

Whenever you feel you've lost sight of what was originally important to you, go back to the beginning and review your goals, mission statement, business plan, and your market research.

You could also hire a manager who may have fresh ideas, and be motivated to take your business in a new direction. The challenge would be to sit back and allow someone else to perform magic with your business. Remember that change is often slow and it may take some time before you see a real turnaround. Employees may have to be replaced, or you may need to remodel or even relocate.

Avoid a Dysfunctional Workplace

The one thing that kills morale and makes stylists walk away is when you have a dysfunctional workplace. Clients often sense when something is wrong and may feel uncomfortable. The worst possible scenario is if clients quit coming to your salon because the tension is so thick. Here are some things to look out for:

1. Unstable relationships

The salon is a competitive business. You are competing with other local salons for business and that fact brings you together as a team. In the same vein, stylists will compete with each other for clients and sales. It's important to have a system in place so that jealousy does not reign out of control. There's nothing that will ruin your business quicker than when stylists are fighting or angry at each other. You can't make them become friends, but they must learn to be accepting of others.

2. Harmful habits

The salon business is demanding. It's hard work and stressful at times. These factors will contribute to your staff's personal way of looking for relief and comfort. This is where alcohol and drugs may play a part. There is no doubt that people need to unwind and will do it in whatever way appeals to them. Let your employees know that alcoholism and drug use will not be tolerated in your salon. Set your boundaries on this topic from the beginning so they know what will happen if they show up for work and are not capable of working.

There are other habits that may be disturbing. Here are some issues that often come up. Employees may be overly distracted with their cell phones, boyfriends/girlfriends or children, leaving the salon to go shopping, constantly eating, or making clients wait too long for their service. Employees may complain too much, gossip or talk only about themselves.

Then there are the 3 things experts say people shouldn't talk about in public: religion, sex and politics. Consider these ideas and decide for yourself how to best handle the situation.

3. Poor organization

It can be frustrating for everyone if your policies are not clear from the start. That's why it's a good practice to put everything in writing. Another area of frustration can be when you offer a promotion to clients and forget to tell your salon coordinator or employees. Keep everyone on the same page and no one will complain about the lack of organization.

4. Lack of confidence

Not everyone has self-confidence or good self-esteem. You must show your best side to both clients and employees. Let them know you are the leader and you lead with confidence and persistence.

There may be a staff member with poor self-esteem. Give encouragement, training and your support. Let staff members know they are valuable to your team, and you believe in their skills. You hired them because you saw something within them, so you must let them know you expect them to live up to your good opinion of them. Most will rise to the occasion and not let you down. Help those who cannot help themselves.

5. Inability to make good decisions

Your clients, employees and salespeople all look to you to make good decisions. Granted, business people do and will make mistakes, but do your best to make smart and informed decisions. Be focused on your business, but not so much that you ignore the needs of your staff. Do your best to not let your private life influence your business life in unfortunate ways. Be clear and focused and you will have a more prosperous future.

6. The owner or manager becomes burned out

The salon business can be particularly stressful, especially when you are wearing so many hats. You may be working behind the chair as a full time stylist, and also managing your salon. Unless you practice excellent stress management techniques, you may find yourself burned out. Burnout is a difficult situation to reverse once it starts. Unmanaged stress can hurt your business, your private life, and your health.

You don't have to suffer through stressful situations. Get some help so you can run your business rather than it running you. There are solutions to too much stress. You may have to cut back on clients, learn to delegate, learn communication strategies, let go of difficult clients or employees, or do whatever is necessary to bring your mental/emotional state back into balance. Take care of yourself, so you can take care of your business.

At one point in my life I experienced sleepless nights or continuous nightmares. Only when I let go of a troublesome employee did the nightmares stop. During my last three years in business I suffered through chronic neck and shoulder pain. Nothing could stop it until I finally let go of the salon. I'm sharing these experiences with you so you understand how stress can affect you if you aren't careful with your thoughts, perceptions and decisions. Look for the signs of stress and do something about it before it gets out of control.

Here are some solutions that helped me: mindfulness-based stress reduction, vacations, hypnosis, a spiritual connection, talking with a counselor, and as a last resort ... medication.

Handling Salon Shrinkage

I prefer to be up front about shrinkage, otherwise known as theft. It's a subject most business owners don't like to think about, but you will eventually have to face this matter. Your business is done predominantly in cash, so it's easy access for sticky fingers. Most employees are honest, but there will occasionally be one who is not. And that one person or persons can do an awful lot of damage to your profit margin. It's very difficult to catch a suspect when every employee has their hands in the cash drawer. The best solution is to have one person, either you or your receptionist, handle all the money.

Ask all staff members to be on the lookout for salon visitors who take products without paying for them. Every stolen item hurts your bottom line.

In Conclusion

There are many ways to ensure your salon is a success. Take care of business and take care of yourself. Read through the guidelines again and make every effort to follow through.

CHAPTER SEVENTEEN
Optimize Retail Sales

Retailing is the sale of goods or articles individually or in small quantities directly to the consumer. Take advantage of this amazing opportunity to sell retail products and substantially increase your profits. To not participate in this lucrative venture is a disservice to your salon, your employees, and your clients. A seminar speaker once said, "with all employees exhibiting sales knowledge, even a small retail area can generate as much profit as one full time employee." That's an incredible opportunity for you, when money is made without having to hire additional staff.

Retail Profitability

Retail sales can generate as much as 25% of salon profit. Your monthly retail profit can be enough to pay your rent or utilities. The products are being used at the back bar and at the stylist's stations, so it makes good sense to support your professional products at the retail level. Sell what you use to make an additional profit. Retail credibility is dependent on you using the same products at both the back bar and on your retail shelves.

Selling your products on the retail market requires you to apply for a state retail license. This license gives you authority from the state to collect sales tax on the products you sell to the public. You in turn send collected tax money to the state either monthly, quarterly, or yearly. Every county has different rules. Also, you may be required to pay a fee for the license. Sometimes the fee is for the life of the business or it can be for a set number of years. Your prospective county or state will inform you of its policies when you apply.

Supplies can be purchased from several different sources. Local beauty supply houses are the easiest. Many have salespeople who travel directly to your salon to take your order, introduce new products, and sometimes deliver your products. Others will require you to travel to them.

Distant suppliers will offer an 800 number for the convenience of ordering from them. Look in the yellow pages or the internet for listings of your local beauty supply houses. If you don't find all of them, don't worry, they will eventually find you.

Many companies will pay shipping costs if you purchase a minimum amount of product and supplies. This is a savings to you. Most supply houses will send you current fliers, catalogs, or newspapers with price quotes and sales. Buy in large quantities during peak times to save money.

Tip: Avoid excessive inventories during slow times of the year, usually January through March, June and July, and September and October. Careful financial planning is the key. You don't want to spend more than about 20% on the dollar for supplies.

Secret: Ask your supply salesperson to separate your supplies into two different receipts: one for your back bar and back room supplies, and the other for your retail products. This will make your bookkeeping easier and you will have a reference as to your expenditures. Taxes will be added to your salon supplies but not your retail products. You will collect those taxes as you sell the products.

Trick: Learn about guaranteed sales. These are the items and products you purchase from beauty supply houses. The deal is if you aren't able to sell the item, you aren't stuck with it. You may return it for credit, but don't wait too long.

Tips for purchasing products and supplies from trade shows:
1. Always get a receipt.
2. Get the company's business card in case you want to re-order an item later.
3. If you can't sell a retail item purchased at a trade show, you might not be able to return it for credit.

Balance Your Inventory

One of the biggest challenges in carrying products for retail and salon use is in balancing inventory. Overstocking product may tie up your funds for some time, and leave you with little or no cash flow. To under stock and run short of products will cause you to lose sales and credibility. While it is always beneficial to purchase products in bulk for a better price, you must keep your purchasing habits in balance. If you are embarking upon a busy season, you may find it necessary to stock up knowing that the products will soon turn over. If a slow season is eminent, you will want to cut down on inventory.

How Revealing Your Clientele Can Also Boost Retail Sales

Know who your target market is to gain the competitive edge. With this information in mind you are ready to establish effective retail strategies. Is your target market young, old, unemployed, employed, affluent, or poor? Are they a particular ethnic group? Get clear because all of these factors will make an impact on your salon's bottom line. Every service you offer and product you sell must be directed toward your target market. Review your business plan and get this information.

Your demographic research gives you vital information regarding the buying habits of your target market. A small retail area is even more profitable when you align your choice of retail products to the needs of that particular clientele. The following example shows how to analyze your retail area, and adapt it to your most lucrative market. This practical information also applies to medium size and larger salons.

Example:

A local salon owner asked me to coach her regarding her retail area. This case study will provide you with ideas of how a less-than-efficient retail area can be made more effective. I'll give you a little history on this salon. Salon X was established mainly as a small, quick cut salon. It had four styling stations, and no room for additional services. The second owner, who we'll call Rachel, later re-established it as a quick cut and a shampoo/set salon. This small salon had no real retail area to speak of, only a small reception space with four chairs squeezed between the desk and the front door. Two short walls on both sides of the waiting area held two small shelving cases, which included a total of nine shelves. Four of them were half the size of the others. The obvious space limitation was a challenge, but not an impossible problem to solve.

The Consultation:

Rachel's current retail system was ineffective in several ways. The first apparent flaw was that the products were not priced. She hadn't taken the time or initiative to price each product or at least put a price near each category. Therefore, no one knew what anything cost. Products without price tags give the impression that they are on display or for show, and not for sale. Many consumers ignore unmarked products. Unmarked products also give buyers the sense that those products are expensive (Just like in a department store).

Rachel's retail area carried only one complete line of products. Only half of another line was for sale, and there were one or two products from six different lines. For instance, there was a gel from one company, mousse from another, one type of shampoo from another, and shampoo and conditioners from another. This sends a very mixed message to the consumer that Rachel actually only believed in one line, and only a few of those products were used on the back bar and at the stylist's stations. Many of the products the stylists used were not for sale to clients. This is not an uncommon situation in many salons.

We took an inventory of Rachel's client base in order to seek more effective retail sales. This information along with her client survey gave us the advantage of up-to-date client feedback. About 30% of the clients were elderly senior citizens, about 40% were male, ages 30 - 60's, and the other 30% were a combination of middle aged women, children, young adults, and a variety of tourists.

The 30% female senior citizens who received weekly shampoo and sets or blow styles never bought anything at the retail level. They would have no need for shampoo and conditioners because of their weekly appointments. My suggestion to Rachel for selling to these elderly women was to carry two hair sprays; a light and a firm hold, one in a can and one with a pump. Some clients have a personal preference toward the can because of the finer spray. These products would be in demand because they support the style during the week between sets. Stylists would be encouraged to use and promote these products.

Male clients made up approximately 40% or more of Rachel's overall clientele. They would sometimes purchase shampoo, conditioners, gel, and mousse. Many men had concerns about thinning hair, so I suggested that Rachel implement a product line that identified and treated thinning hair problems. I also recommended a newer line of products designed specifically for men.

The final 30% of clients were a mix of children, tourists, and women between the ages of 25 and 50. Retail sales to this group were moderate because the staff did not promote retail products.

In preparing a strategy for retail profitability, I analyzed several factors. The neighborhood was fairly affluent so there was room to trade up on product prices. The next step was to find out what the competition was retailing. I recommend selling products that differed from the competition. Why would anyone go specifically to Rachel's salon to purchase products if they could buy them anywhere?

All excess products could be returned for credit or be marked down for a quick resale.

Altogether, I suggested that product lines be narrowed down to no more than two for the general public; one low priced, one upscale priced, and two for Rachel's lucrative men's market. Rachel made the changes and saw increased retail sales.

Tip: The secret here is that retail products and prices must be in alignment with the salon's service prices. If the client's service ticket is $10-15, they aren't going to pay $20 for a bottle of shampoo. A small variation of low and higher priced products would be most advantageous. This gives clients with discretionary income the opportunity to trade up.

When Rachel is ready to launch her marketing campaign she could take the following actions:

- Target a large former clientele by going through files and sending postcards to past clients.
- Target local motels in a heavy tourist zone.
- Target the upscale neighborhood in which she is located. Flyers, neighborhood newspapers, and business cards were used as a promotion strategy.

Encourage Clients to Buy

Encourage your clients to purchase their hair, skin, and nail products from you rather than from the department or drug store.

Let them know they won't get the salon look and feel if they don't use the salons' products.

Tip: Many salons won't guarantee the success of their permanent waves if the client doesn't use the salon's specially formulated shampoos and conditioners. It just makes sense.

Your Salesperson Can Help You Sell

Ask your distributor salesperson or company representative to visit your salon and teach your staff how to use and sell their products. Trade shows are also a good place to receive product education. Notice how products are sold from the platform. Direct the same selling techniques to educate your stylists and clients.

The 7 Principles of Great Retailing

1. Use your window or display shelves to display and advertise products and on-going sales. If properly displayed, most products sell themselves. All you have to do is use them and mention their benefits.

2. Make your retail products available to the client. Allow them to touch the products, notice the professional packaging, read the labels, and smell inside the bottles.

3. Promote a sense of professionalism by selling products that come equipped with their own Point of Purchase displays. POP displays are attractive, professional and increase your profits.

4. The keys to retail success:
   - Never display or purchase one of anything.
   - Keep your retail shelves fully stocked at all times. Show that you have confidence in the products you sell.

- Create an illusion of more. You can place mirrors behind product shelves to give the illusion of quantity.
- Sales are lost by not paying attention to inventory. Purchase enough product.
- Always keep your retail shelves clean and each product individually priced.
- Make sure your merchandising displays are fresh and professional looking.

5. Rotate products within the salon selling areas. The desk is the most high profile area, so display new products and impulse items there first, then rotate them to other areas. Be careful not to oversupply the desk. If it looks too cluttered, clients will regard the products as junk.

6. Follow the good business strategies of department and grocery stores by offering a range of products at different price points. Your products would appeal to a wider audience, and capture the clientele who purchase their products at discount stores. You then have the opportunity for the client to up-grade to better and more expensive products within your salon.

Another tip I got from grocery stores: put discount priced items in a SALE basket. People love sales and they love to search for treasures.

7. Use your new products to run special promotions every month. If you run out of new products to promote, then re-promote the older products in a new way called packaging. Package a shampoo and conditioner together, or a finishing rinse and conditioner, or products for chemically treated hair. Put a slow seller along with a new product. Consider packaging a special brush or cosmetic mirror along with a product or two.

Use various combinations and find ways to get slow moving products out of the salon. Think profit. It affects your bottom line.

Review Your Salon's Retail Image

Take a long hard look at the front of your salon, not as the owner, but as a client. Try to see through the client's eyes, and be objective on the appearance of your retail areas. Ask a friend to give you honest feedback. Ask yourself these important questions:

1. Does your reception/retail area look inviting?
2. Would you be motivated to spend your money here?
3. Is everything behind glass or is it touchable? Protecting merchandise from clients delivers the message don't touch, which can be mentally transferred to "don't buy, this stuff is just to look at."
4. Are the brands recognizable or are they obscure?
5. Are the products priced, clean and dusted, and orderly?
6. Is there a substantial quantity on the shelf?
7. Is there someone there to answer questions and collect money?
8. Are there bags available (with your logo on them) to carry away products?

Remember that most products sell themselves and offer an attractive profit potential. The downside of retail is that everything presented on open shelves eventually needs to be dusted, which is time consuming and bothersome. The small amount of effort expended on cleanliness is well worth the trouble.

Recount Retail Sales

At the end of the week, the receptionist and your computer software should be able to give you valuable information: how much you've done in retail sales, which stylist sold the most products, which brand name sold the most products, and which products are most asked for by clients.

Predicting Retail Sales

There are two suggested ways of predicting sales and estimating profit margins. The first is to pinpoint your target market and supply what they will buy, or you can estimate the total market and then predict your businesses' expected market penetration. It could be difficult to do this and the figures may be unrealistic.

I suggest selling products that you believe in and use. Products that perform extremely well for your stylists will also perform for the client. The fact that you stand behind them will encourage your clients to try them, and that strengthens repeat business.

Product Shrinkage

Salon owners express a concern about the safety of retail products. Many salon owners refuse to carry retail products because they are afraid that employees and shoplifters will steal the merchandise. You're right, they will. Only you can decide if retailing is worth it or not.

Most shopping centers have a system whereby each merchant calls to warn one another of people shoplifting within the center. The merchant who catches them must call the police. If your salon is independent of a shopping center, then you must decide how to handle shoplifters when you catch them. Will you prosecute? What if it's someone you know, a regular client or worse ... an employee? Decide on a procedure when setting policies.

Tip: Boxes containing cosmetics, curling irons, diffusers and other products are a target for shoplifters. They may appear untouched, but this can be deceiving. When cleaning my salon I would occasionally find empty boxes. Then it's too late to do anything about it. You just can't watch everybody and everything all the time. Ask your employees to be alert and not make it easy for shoplifters. Call the police immediately if you catch someone.

Tip: Female clients sometimes leave their purses lying around, especially near the door in the reception area. Politely ask these clients to keep their purses with them. Keep an eye on fur coats or expensive items.

Keeping your insurance policy up to date is recommended. Most policies have a $500 - $1,000 deductible, so you may end up paying for stolen items out of your pocket.

How to Price Your Products

There are standard practices for pricing merchandise. Care should be taken in order to be fair and not price gouge. Below are some ways in which you may price your products for the marketplace:

1. Pricing based on cost: calculate your cost and add over head and commissions.

2. Add a suggested manufacturer percentage: cost plus 30-50% or more. Subtract 10% commissions to employees off the top.

3. Calculate your overhead by figuring the square footage of your retail area and volume of product and turnover of product.

4. Certain products will have a fixed price to charge. Your profit margin increases as you purchase products at bulk rates or on sale.

5. Competitive pricing: determine what the competition is charging for the product and follow suit.

6. Decide what the market will bear: determine what the customer will pay for the product and charge accordingly.

I won a case of shampoo at a large trade show. I was not familiar with the brand, but it appeared to be a good product. I put a low price on it to move it, but still had a difficult time selling it because there was no product recognition and no education. Even a low price point failed to attract clients. I sold all the product, but it took time and space. The most challenging part of retailing in a small area is having enough available space for everything you would like to sell. You need to pick and choose.

How to Choose Between Brand Name and Private Label Products

Brand Name 'Professional only' Products

Professional only are products such as shampoos, conditioners, hair sprays, mousses, permanent waves, hair color, etc., which are produced by specialized companies which formulate their products to be used only under the supervision of a licensed cosmetologist. They are never intended to be sold to discount stores, drug stores or department stores. They are used exclusively by salon owners. It is my belief that the most superior companies develop their products through intensive scientific research to bring the professional hairstylist the very best hair and skin care products on the market today. Salon owners complain that they can't compete with mass markets for price, however, you have the advantage when you compete with proven quality products and expert product knowledge.

There are many, many brand name 'professional only' products from which to choose. My advice is to investigate and try as many as possible. Most stylists learn about products from various salons in which they worked. Experience is the best teacher. I have found that most products are good, so it's a matter of personal preference. You'll need to narrow down the competition because you certainly can't afford to purchase them all. You will find that brand name products have unique, attractive packaging. A great deal of research goes into the package design and product development.

Education, research knowledge support and national advertising are important tools for sales and profits. Some companies offer co-op advertising to save you money.

"Some of the disadvantages of brand name products are that many stylists don't get enough satisfaction from the products."

They can't find a line that exactly works for them. Some brand name products can be expensive and are not competitive with discount and drug store products. No matter how good the products are, some clients will not spend the money. They might once but not twice because they will not notice a difference from less expensive brands. There are so many lines that the client, as well as the stylist, is confused. Many stylists complain about finding their professional products in drug stores, sometimes at a lesser price. Brand name products are generally pre-priced and the average mark-up is about 30-50%, sometimes more.

Private Label Products

Some salons choose private label products over brand name. These salons feel that they have more control over their retailing program. They can have products made to their specifications. Ordering from a private label company can keep prices down, and eliminate some of the time salon owners spend with salespeople and the paper work involved. There is a certain amount of prestige involved in having a salon's own line of products, and the client must return to the salon in order to purchase the product.

Your own private label can build and reinforce your salon image. It can also protect you from product diversion. There's no reason to be concerned that the products you worked so hard to promote will be found on the discount store shelves.

Private label companies coordinate packaging for both hair care and skin care lines. They introduce new products several times a year and sometimes have a newsletter and business guides to keep you informed.

What to look for in private label products:

1. A manufacturer who offers quality products. Investigate the quality of their products before you put your name on the bottle. Be certain they have a good reputation in the industry and are financially solid. Ask for a list of current users, and call them for an interview.

2. Ask if they carry products for many different hair types. Ingredients make a difference.

3. Ask if they continually add new products to the line?

4. Is everything prepared in-house? Will they be able to help you with packaging, research and development, custom fragrances, domestic and international product restrictions and regulations,

shipping etc? The delays may be long if they contract the work out. You may also hire a graphic designer to design your labels.

5. Offering a variety of packaging options will give your brand more versatility. You will also need products for the back bar.

6. After choosing to retail private label products, you must set prices, merchandise the products, and train your staff to sell them. The prices of your products must be attractive to the client, while still maintaining a quality image. Attractive displays, in-salon advertising, and point-of-purchase materials can substantially increase profitability.

However, all the advertising in the world won't sell your product in-salon unless your staff reinforces the message. They must educate the client about the advantages of custom-made products.

The Disadvantages of Private Label Products

The disadvantages are that you may only sell products to your regular customers, those to whom you have recommended the products. The private label company will supply information, and may or may not supply education. That could be difficult for employees who need motivation in order to sell. You will be responsible for educational classes. All the advertising is in your hands. There will be no national name recognition, no national television and magazine advertisements and no co-op agreements. It is also difficult to compete with the technology of brand name products. You are also required to purchase a minimum order.

Retail Questionnaire

1. What products would you like your stylists to sell more of? What key benefits do you feel will entice customers to buy?

Product #1_____ Key benefits_____

Product #2_____ Key benefits_____

Product #3_____ Key benefits_____

Product #4_____ Key benefits_____

Product #5_____ Key benefits_____

Product #6_____ Key benefits_____

2. What services would you like your staff members to promote?

3. Your clientele consists mainly of:

Gender _____

Income range _____

Occupations _____

Outside interests/hobbies/concerns _____

4. What situations or staff insecurities are currently holding them back from selling more?

Stylist #1_____

Stylist #2_____

Stylist #3 _____

Stylist #4 _____

5. Ideally, what amount of product sales or services sales would you like each stylist to be earning?

6. What incentives have you used in the past to encourage your stylists to stretch and make more sales?

Teach Employees How to Sell

In order to retail successfully, staff members must first be taught the importance of *how* and *why* to do it. Teach employees how good retailing and good customer relations serves the client and the salon at the same time. Clients have their products, the employee makes a sales commission and the salon makes a profit to stay in business. Education and product knowledge is necessary for growth.

Develop a positive attitude in your salon about retailing. When employees notice your eagerness to sell and make additional money, they too will be motivated to get in on this extra benefit. Help fearful staff members over their fear of selling and rejection. Explain that they are doing your clients a favor by introducing them to new products and educating them about products that maintain their cut, style or chemical service over time. Drug store products can't compete with the quality and science behind many professional products. Don't lose sales to drug stores and mass market discount stores who know nothing about the products or personal service.

Exercise: Role play for retail products

Let your staff meetings be opportunities to role play. One person can be a client and another the staff member. Develop a script about your new product and let each staff member take turns promoting the item and asking for the sale. Let another person be the client who raises questions or concerns about the product. This is a good exercise to learn about a new product, increase sales and serve your clients.

Staff Member Questionnaire

1. What products do you believe in and use on your own hair?

2. What products do your clients currently buy and use?

3. What key benefits excite your clients to currently buy these products?

4. What key benefits do you feel will entice customer to buy?

Product #1_____ Key benefits_____

Product #2_____ Key benefits_____

Product #3_____ Key benefits_____

Product #4_____ Key benefits_____

5. What services do your clients currently prefer?

6. What are the key benefits of these services that excite clients to want them?

Service #1_____   Benefit #1_____ Benefit #2_____
                              Benefit #3_____

Service #2 _____   Benefit #1_____ Benefit #2_____
                              Benefit #3_____

Service#3 _____   Benefit #1 _____ Benefit #2_____
                              Benefit #3_____

Service#4 _____   Benefit #1 _____ Benefit #2_____
                              Benefit #3_____

7. From noticing your client's preferences, what products and benefits would appeal to them?

8. How do you sell products now?

9. Do you use them on the client during the visit?

10. Do you refer to the hair problems your client mentioned during the initial consultation?

11. What situations make you feel uneasy and hold you back from selling more?

12. Have you ever had any sales training? What did you learn?

13. How do you feel about asking for the sale? Comfortable or fearful? Please explain:

14. Describe a time when a salesperson helped you understand the benefits of a product or service, and subsequently you were happy you bought the product or invested in the service:

Product:_____

Why you were happy? _____

15. How did the salesperson help you make a good decision?

16. Ideally, what amount of product sales or services sales would you like to be earning?

17. Name some difficult things you have accomplished in the past:

18. How did you push yourself to try new things or do something that felt uncomfortable?

19. Did you reward yourself?

20. Did you keep score of your progress?

21. What do you feel would excite you to ask for more sales?

22. What would you do with about $600.00 more per month when you increase your product and services sales?

23. How would you have more enjoyment in your life, with an additional $600.00 per month?

In Conclusion

Optimizing retail sales benefits everyone. The client has a professional product that supports their service, and time is saved by one-stop shopping. The employee successfully represented the product and salon during the sale and made a commission. The salon owner receives satisfaction from the sale as well as profits. It's a win-win situation.

Notes:

CHAPTER EIGHTEEN
Market Your Salon for
BIG Success

Every entrepreneur will find it necessary to market his or her business venture, whether it's brand new or has been established for many years. A hair salon is no different. Salon marketing coordinates your business activities in order to attract potential clients. This will include advertising, promotion, and public relations. You'll also include internet marketing. In the early stages of salon development, you will need to effectively position your salon in the public eye. Develop a savvy plan and identify your salon as superior in its category.

The cost of doing business increases yearly as rents increase, product prices accelerate, utilities skyrocket and advertising costs escalate. In order to cut costs, many salon owners reduce the money they spend toward marketing. This detrimental practice only decreases the flow of new clients into the salon. Salon owners are faced with the challenge of increasing income and volume in order to maintain profitability. Here are some solutions to this problem.

Ten Steps to Better Marketing

Marketing is not an exact science, but there are some predetermined steps and strategies that marketing experts use to help entrepreneurs get ahead in business. These ten steps will put you at an advantage because you will know what others do not or will not take the time to learn. It's not difficult, in fact you probably already have the necessary skills to become an expert marketer. Think back to all the ways you've ever been successful at anything in life, and you will see that you have what it takes to make your salon a booming success.

Step 1. Choose Your Primary Objective

Your primary objective is the one thing or goal you would like to accomplish this year. You will most likely achieve that goal through your marketing efforts.

For your marketing plan, what are your first guesses as to where you want to be?

One year?

Two years?

Five years?

The general public is aware that there are many great salons and great hair stylists. So it becomes difficult to prove that one is any better than another. The one thing you can do to stand apart from the crowd is to emphasize what you do that is truly different or unique in your community. We talked about that in *Chapter Five: Identify Your Competition*, and it's just as important to your marketing plan. Look back at what you wrote to refresh your mind.

Active marketing is the best and only way to promote your uniqueness. Word of mouth is great, but it's rather slow, so promotion is critical. If you are the first salon to implement a new service, then you may create a new market, otherwise you will be sharing from an existing market.

Exercise: Of the goals you want to accomplish this year, ask yourself these questions: is it new, is it unique and will it help me to stand out?

Educate Yourself in Business Principles

One of the most proactive things you can do to promote your business is to read business success books: marketing, sales, promotion, publicity, advertising, copywriting, and persuasion. The Chamber of Commerce and the Small Business Administration offer many classes in business management and social media. They offer either free or inexpensive literature. Bookstores, libraries, and newsstands carry an incredible amount of helpful business information. Well-known entrepreneurs are willing to share the powerful secrets of their success, so you have the opportunity to learn from the pros. I have my own library of success and motivational books and programs. Sometimes all we need is a little positive reinforcement.

Step 2. Know Who You Are

Why did you go into business? This is just one of the many questions you need to ask yourself while you are defining your image and setting up your marketing campaign. It's crucial that you know who you are and how you are different from other salons in your community. What special needs does your business meet? Are you offering services or products not available anywhere else? What can you do or offer that will make your salon unique? What is outstanding about your staff? What problems does your professional team solve? How will your clients benefit psychologically? What are your specialties, areas of expertise and how will your clients benefit from all of this?

What service or product is especially unique to your business?

How do you choose which services or products to promote? Always consider where is the best opportunity for profit, and which market areas hold the most potential for growth? Try a brand new product from your suppliers or perhaps an imported line that is exclusive to you. Develop and promote a product for your target market. You may have some overstocked merchandise to sell on clearance. Attracting people to sale items gets them into your salon. They'll see who you are and maybe even make a service appointment.

In your promotional material, you must define what you do and explain the benefits to the client. Remember, it's about educating the client and guiding them to trust you. You must ask yourself the following questions:

1. Why am I in this business?
2. How do I distinguish myself from the competition?
3. What am I trying to achieve with this promotion?
4. What goal am I trying to achieve this year?
5. What are my strategies for accomplishing these results?
6. What benefits do I offer the client?

Step 3. Investigate Your Competitors

An important part of any marketing plan is to determine which salons are competing for the same target market. In *Chapter Five, Identify Your Competition* you made a detailed study of all the competitive salons in the community where you plan to open a salon. Maybe you are looking to expand your salon or move to another location and need this critical data. Go back to that chapter and review your notes.

Get data from your research to find salons with a comparable image and price point. If not, ask your co-workers about competitive salons. They may have worked for them at one time. They may have friends or former school mates who are working in one, or who own competing salons. Friends, family, and neighbors are also a good source of information. Ask your clients about their former salons. Your distributor salespeople are also a good source of information about salons with an image similar to yours. Don't be shy ... ask!

All salons will be listed in the phone book or on the internet. Notice the size of their yellow pages ad if they have one. They pay a lot for a large ad. Pay attention to your competitors' newspaper advertising and how often they place ads. Who uses billboard advertising?

> **"Take steps to find out crucial information. Discover the details: the atmosphere of the salon, how large it is, how many employees they have, what services they offer, their fee structure, educational requirements, and any unique characteristics which set them apart from other salons in your community."**

Finally, analyze your information and be aware of how you do or don't measure up. Is there a standard that you aren't meeting? Is there something more you can do, but are afraid to take a risk? Maybe you are the most innovative, trend setting, efficiently run salon in your area? Maybe the most popular, creative stylists work for you?

Maybe you are new to the scene, and just out of beauty school. This research will help you choose a salon to work in and learn the ropes. It's great experience. I worked in the best, most elegant salon in my hometown. I quit six years later to open my own new, improved, updated and professional salon. I knew exactly what to do and what not to do and I never looked back.

Step 4. Identify Your Target Market

We've talked about your target market throughout this book and by now you should have lots of information regarding who they are and what they want. You'll use that information now to put together your marketing campaign.

Demographics are: age, income level, culture, hobbies, vacations, lifestyle factors, and children. Do you know how much money your target market spends on products or services relating to your business? You may be able to find out that information from trade magazines or on the internet. Use key words to pinpoint the exact information you want.

Are your client's senior citizens, children, teenagers, single adults, high school or college students or families? Do your potential clients work in an industrial park where you may soon open a business? Are they employed with a large disposable income or do they depend upon their parents for their spending money? You may notice a cross-section or a very specific group. We defined your target market earlier. What did you learn?

A new salon can define their customer before they open their doors, because they've placed their doors right in the middle of their target market.

Tip: The purpose of defining your target market is not to limit your potential market, but to focus your energy and resources where it will best be served.

Choosing several suitable markets is a good way in which to expand your clientele. The more you know about your potential clients, the better equipped you will be to direct your promotional efforts. If you want to make a radical change in your salon and your clientele, you may have to close up, remodel and open a brand new salon. Some owners even hire all new staff.

A friend and I drove to a town in Northern California to visit our friend for Thanksgiving weekend. We were to meet at a local grocery store. While waiting for our friend I couldn't help but notice all the overweight people who came in and out of the store. I was convinced a weight loss clinic would be a great business in that town. When I mentioned it to our friend, she agreed and informed us that Curves (the thirty minute exercise system) was doing a booming business. I was not surprised. This story is a good example of noticing the obvious demographics in your town or area. Hang out a while and be observant.

Demographics and Lifestyle Factors

Demographic (statistics) and lifestyle factors are the two areas to analyze. Lifestyle factors are special interest activities, philosophical beliefs, social factors and cultural involvements. You can find this information through your local Chamber of Commerce and also on the internet through the most current Census. Having this information could be helpful if your target market is an ethnic population.

Step 5. Determine Your Position

One of the key marketing principles is called positioning. It is important to determine exactly what niche you intend to fill. Your position in the community differentiates you from competitive salons. Decide what kind of impression you want to present to the public? Write it out on paper and repeat it back to yourself. Does it sound right? Does it sound comfortable?

Does it sound true? Take some time to think this step through. Positioning is vital to the success of your promotional efforts.

Ask yourself these questions about positioning:
1. Will you position your salon as having the best colorists?
2. Will you position your salon as the go-to place for quick haircuts?
3. Will you position your salon as the upscale salon in town?
4. Will you position your salon as the go-to place to be pampered?
5. What position will you fill in the minds of your community? Decide right at the beginning if possible so you can deliver that message to your community.

Tip: Now that you've positioned yourself in the business community, be certain that this image aligns with your salon image and the caliber of employee you hire.

Step 6. Create a Strategy

You know who you are and what you are good at. You know your niche. You know who the competition is and what they are doing. You know who your client is and what they want. Your next step is to pull all this information together and develop a strategy for success. When we are children, we learn to play games and sports in school. It is our first experience with executing a strategy and a plan to win the game. We know the competition's weaknesses and their strengths. It works the same way in the marketplace. With that information we develop a strategy and map out the most direct and efficient way to success.

The world's most successful corporations are where they are today because someone has vision or foresight. They see what is possible. Secondly, they plan every step of the way. They plan their entry into the competitive marketplace armed with ways to attract their chosen clients and if necessary, pull them away from the competition.

Think through your intentions. Once your intentions are written down, you are ready for the planning stages. Review your goals from a previous chapter. Your goals take on a sense of reality when you can see the overall picture. Since many goals are complex, they might need to be divided into smaller steps. It then becomes easier to identify what needs to be accomplished. Upgrade or adjust them when necessary.

> **"Pay attention to your priorities and take the most important actions. Those will be the actions that take you closest to realizing your dream salon."**

Following a well thought out strategy can keep you moving forward in the direction of accomplishment. Undoubtedly, some ideas may or may not work. That's okay, it happens. You move on to your next promotion. The idea behind strategic planning is to keep you on course. You'll soon learn what promotions work and which ones don't.

The key is to know your target market and what they want. We explored that question many times. If you don't know … ask! Talk to clients and ask what they want. They'll tell you. With that information, you choose the media that most easily reaches them. It's not an exact science. Over time you'll get a better feel for what works and what doesn't. You could start with free media first: publicity and press releases. Get good word of mouth advertising. Ask good clients to tell their friends and family about you. Then move forward with paid promotions and advertising.

Keep in mind that you will have many options from which to choose. If you do your market research and demographic analysis, you may come up with more than one direction in which to take your business. Don't settle on one until you've explored many variations. The simple way may or may not be the most lucrative. That is why you must carefully evaluate obvious changes: in the industry, in what services are in demand, in neighborhoods, and in the economy.

Always have a back up plan in case your original plan doesn't work out. Businesses of all sizes have failures. It happens. They let go and move on to a more successful idea.

Network Marketing - Build a Network of Allies

As the salon owner, manager, or staff member, you are in a unique networking position. You have many clients frequenting your salon who can be advocates for your business. Word of mouth is the best form of advertisement and also flattery. Your clients have friends, family, co-workers and acquaintances, all potential supporters of your business. Vigorously market to these clients. Hand out your business cards to everyone. Serve them well, and the business will return to you.

Your clients come from all walks of life and have a vast array of life experiences. They may have contacts that could open doors for you. You could have access to resources formerly not available to you or anyone else. Remember to think strategically, and always develop fair, honest, and respectful relationships with your clients. People like to help people that they like and trust. Keep an open mind.

Educate the Public

The major portion of marketing a service business is educational in nature. You will educate the public as to what exactly your salon does, how it's different from the others, and the advantages of utilizing your services. Be clear in communicating your message both verbally and in all media: newspaper, brochure, radio, web site, blog, Facebook, LinkedIn, Twitter, press releases and promotions.

Step 7. Establish Your Budget

How much money do you invest in marketing your salon? Business planners suggest that a new enterprise spend about 10% of their business's gross revenues on marketing during the first year in operation. Implement a reduction of 5% the second year, then leveling off around 3% per year after that. Hair salons generally spend about 1.2¢ on the dollar or more. Be prepared to invest whatever is required to make an impression and to be valued, which may be more or less than the suggested costs. If you have a small budget, you may need to find inexpensive, creative ways to promote yourself.

Two of the main goals of promotion for all businesses is to increase sales, and secondly to establish who you are and what you have to offer to the community. Don't be afraid to put money in this important area. Spend your money intelligently, and it will certainly return with salon growth, boosted sales figures, and rising profits.

Step 8. Create Your Communication Messages: Create an Identity System

Go to a graphic designer or advertising agency and ask them to design an outdoor sign, if you need one, and a logo for your business. Your logo or graphic identity should communicate what your business is all about. It's a powerful media and marketing tool that defines your uniqueness.

When you are developing your identity system, remember to keep a consistent look and feel for visual similarity. For effective name recognition, use the same symbols or images on all your printed materials and internet marketing.

Logo

It's critical to the success of the logo to keep it in line with your company image. Some businesses prefer to use abstract symbols. Others prefer a stylized rendition of their names or a combination of both. Whichever style you choose to make that first good impression, choose a design which is simple, eye catching, and easy to remember.

Use your logo on everything from stationary to shopping bags, receipts, signs, flyers, labels etc., and in all your advertising. When people see it they will identify it with you and your business.

Have the designer check to be sure the logo is not already being used, or that yours is not uncomfortably close to a corporate identity. There are trademark restrictions, so be careful about what you choose.

You can find inexpensive graphic designers on the internet (Craig's List) who can design nice logos. Look at their web site portfolios before you commit to anything.

Do It Yourself Graphic Design

If your budget is small, you could also do your graphic design on a home computer. Buy and study books on brochure design. You don't have to go out and hire an artist to get quality graphic elements. Excellent illustrations already exist and are readily available from clip-art vendors on the internet. I've used www.clipart.com and www.bigstock.com. Images help set the mood or tone of the brochure or web site. Place original images (photographs) on a page by first scanning them into your computer, then into your page layout program.

A copy store or service bureau can scan your photos for a nominal fee, which varies according to color and resolution. When it comes to printing, your local printer can make suggestions within your budget. Take your ideas to them in the early stages of development so you don't waste time and effort designing a brochure too expensive to print. It is also possible to photocopy your materials for short runs. It's more economical to have materials printed for longer runs over 1,000.

Trick: Keep delivery costs in mind. The heavier paper weight will add to the cost of mailing a large amount of brochures.

Salon Menu

Create a menu which lists the descriptions and prices of all your services. Place it at your desk where clients can see it, or behind the desk on the wall. Make it attractive and large enough to read.

Your Business Card

Design a professional looking business card with your name, address, and phone number on it. You may also want to include your email address and your web site. Try to capture the essence of your salon image. Create a design that will appeal to your target market.

Add your logo or slogan if you have one, and any pertinent information about your salon. On the reverse side of the card you could reserve space for the date and time of the client's next appointment or your hours of operation. Print enough to have on hand for a while, and also enough to give to your employees. Don't purchase a real large quantity in the beginning, in case you decide to change your design or information.

You can also purchase inexpensive business cards from a

stationary store to run through your printer. They are preprinted and perforated with a colorful design. You can also get matching envelopes, letterheads, tri-fold brochures, and postcards.

Express to your employees the importance of being generous with your business cards. Give them to everyone they meet. Keep a stack handy on your desk and at all employee work stations.

Create a Dazzling Brochure

Your brochure is an effective promotional tool whose purpose is to inform and motivate. Brochures are a bit more complicated to design than a flyer or a newspaper advertisement, but they quickly and succinctly give your clients the most important information they need to know about you. Here is a list of items to include:

- Show things happening by using two or three action photos.
- Use a single visual on the cover.
- Describe in your copy how the client will benefit from your products and services.
- Tell readers what problems you can solve, and what results they can expect.
- Provide credentials, if possible: Include contests you have won.
- Use quotes from satisfied clients
- Highlight the specialties of your staff
- Include success stories
- Include any guarantees which you might offer
- Use at least one of these proven power words: "improve, discover, you, free, health, guarantee, new, proven, safety, save and money."
- Your copy must be easy to read.

- Include a map if your salon is particularly difficult to find.
- If you use charts, keep them simple.
- Keep the same visual elements and tone as the rest of your promotional efforts.

Make sure that your brochure appeals to the needs of your target market, and establishes credibility. Your brochure must be attractive, believable, and provide a call for action. Be certain that your name, address, phone number, email address and web site are included. You may also want to include your Facebook fan page and how they can follow you on Twitter. Add the hours you are open. I recommend putting your prices on an insert page. That way when your prices increase you can replace the insert, not the entire brochure.

There are two approaches you can take with your brochure: the subtle approach and the direct approach. With a subtle approach you are laying a foundation for future contacts with the client. A direct approach relies on the client to make the next move by taking advantage of your offer, coupon, postcard etc.

Tip: Get at least three bids for your design work. Plan ahead for printed materials, and you'll get better production and controlled costs. Designers charge extra for last minute rush jobs. Allow ample time for each phase of the process: designing, copywriting, photography, retouching, typesetting, proofreading, printing and bindery work.

Order your paper early enough so that it is available by the time your job is ready for the printer. Ask the designer to assist you in choosing a paper stock that will print well with your favorite typeface, illustrations or photography. Constantly check on how your job is progressing, and include time for corrections. Read your copy carefully, because after a certain point it becomes expensive and troublesome to correct any content or spelling errors.

Promotions

Promotion is about letting the public know you exist so you can cultivate a thriving business. You are promoting your services and products to your target market and making a favorable impression on the community. Typical promotions for the salon are: any service at a reduced price, a new service, a new product, a new employee, an open house, an anniversary, or any type of celebration. The results of promotion are to attract a strong customer base and an excellent professional reputation.

It is a good idea to plan your promotions at the beginning of each year. This practice prevents you from forgetting to do it during busy times. I suggest going through your calendar before the Christmas Holiday and planning exactly the events you want to promote that following year. Don't throw a promotion package together quickly at the last minute without much thought as to it's content and effectiveness. Mistakes can occur, costing you money and your reputation.

Poor planning or underestimating a sales potential may cause you to lose sales. Don't embarrass your salon by not having enough sale items on hand when you need them.

Ask yourself some critical questions about the promotions you offer to your target market:

1. Are your promotions realistic?

2. Do your promotions fit into your budget?

3. Are your promotions unique?

4. Can you make a profit?

5. Are your promotions in alignment with previous ones?

List your first ideas for several targeted promotions:

1.
2.
3.
4.
5.
6.

* In the beginning, it may be trial and error. Be aware of what you could do differently that might contribute to your success.

Tip: You will need to post a sign in your salon if you run more than one promotion at a time saying 'only one discount per visit.' Do at least one promotion every month. You can never have too much business. Put up another sign in your salon which states satisfaction guaranteed and mean it.

Advertise for Success

Advertising attracts attention to the salon and creates the most favorable impression on the public. It expands the growth and development of your salon business. It's a sales proposition in which you are getting the consumers attention to mentally involve them with your product or service. Provide information they want. Present a problem to which you have the solution. Present a situation with which they can identify.

Tip: For effective advertising you must pinpoint your target market, state the problem, list the benefits or state why the client should use your service or purchase your product, support your claims, and ask for the sale.

The Rules for Effective Advertising

1. Be single-minded. Don't dilute your efforts by going in too many directions.
2. Have an overall plan. Keep your salon, its image, and your advertising all on the same wavelength. Be focused. Don't try to be all things to all people.
3. Make a meaningful promise to the consumer. The promise is a summary statement and lists the benefits of the product or service.
4. Be sensitive to changes in the marketplace. Change your strategy and your products when necessary.
5. Remember that quality sells. You must provide true value to the client in order for them to want to purchase your products. Value is a combination of price and quality.

Coupons

Coupons are a draw for many people, especially for those who have an aversion to paying full price. Put them in newspapers and coupon booklets, or distribute them individually. You can put them in the shopping bag along with retail purchases. Two for the price of one coupons are successful, as well as "Get $5.00 off on a $50.00 purchase."

Secret: Check first before putting your coupons on windshields in a parking lot. Some towns have an ordinance against littering and the police could charge you a fine.

Newspaper Advertisements

Your local newspapers can help your reach potential clients. Sign a long-term contract and you will get a better rate. (The following information is also useful for designing your brochure and web site.)

Tips on writing an advertisement:

- Appeal to the client's self-interest or state some news.
- It is beneficial to personalize the headline and offer a benefit.
- Use simple layouts.
- Avoid a cluttered ad, too many photos, and multiple typefaces.
- Your ad will look better if you use variations of one singular typeface such as bold, italic and roman rather than multiple typefaces (use a classic typeface such as Helvetica, Times Roman, Garamond, Arial or Futura).
- The illustration is usually more important than the headline.
- A dramatic or outstanding photo or illustration with a brand name can deliver a clear message without the use of a headline or copy.
- Photos work better than artwork and offer compelling visual evidence.
- A caption under the photo gets twice as much readership as body copy.
- A picture with a caption can be an advertisement unto itself.
- When writing your copy, make it easy to read.
- Use upper and lower case letters for the text, never all caps.
- San serif type is best for headlines and display type, while serif type provides easy readability for the text.

This is Serif Type (Palatino)
This is Sans Serif Type (Helvetica)

Print media can deliver impact, and be as creative in its form as in its content.

An advertising agency or your newspaper's sales representative can guide you in your advertising campaign. Due to the rising costs of advertising, it is always a smart decision to consult with a qualified professional before launching your campaign. You want your newspaper advertisements to achieve three goals:

1. Impress the public with your image
2. Grab their attention
3. Motivate them to call you

Secret: Don't neglect your local high school or college newspapers. Their prices are often very reasonable and you can attract a lot of young people. They do care about maintaining their image. Many youth have good paying jobs and a disposable income. A satisfied teenager is a great advertisement. They will generate a lot of excitement about your salon and are eager to tell their friends about you.

Public Relations

Public relations is all about keeping the public informed and interested in your business. It encompasses all the activities you do to obtain free exposure for your business. Some examples of PR are press releases, announcements, feature stories, interviews, and press conferences.

Local newspapers and radio stations write interviews and feature stories about local business leaders. Readers enjoy personal interest stories. You could write your own light personal interest story and send it to the features editor of your local newspaper.

Press Release

Press releases are a good way to begin with public relations. It is designed to release information about your salon business. Write a press release for newsworthy major events: the opening of your new salon, a new location, an award you or an employee has won, or new additional staff members. You need a unique angle or a strong purpose in order to be noticed by the editor. It must contain information about something new, interesting, and of benefit to the public.

A well-written presentation is important. The press release format consists of source information, the release date, a headline, the body and conclusion. Use your letterhead stationary, and make your presentation simple and easy to read.

The standard format is double-spaced paragraphs with a contact person listed in the top right corner of the page. You should limit your release to one page. The six basic elements which will get your message across are: who, what, when, where, why, and how of your major event. Make sure the information is grammatically correct. Many newspapers and radio stations have guidelines for a standard press release. Call to request the information.

After your press release is written, send it to a specific person:

- Call the city editor at the newspaper office. Ask them how much lead time is necessary before it is printed. Get it to them on time.
- The news director at the radio station.
- The assignment desk for television news shows.

Press Kit

Many business owners create a press kit. Included in this 9 X 12 packet of information is the press release, photographs, articles about you and your expertise, your brochure, a business card and any other pertinent information. Include an energetic cover letter to capture the editor's attention. It could possibly get you either a live or phone interview.

Be sure to mail it on time, or deliver it to the editor yourself. Call the editor several days before the event to be certain he or she received your packet. Ask if you could answer any questions or comments at that time. Don't give up if you don't get noticed the first time. Continue to send releases until you receive the exposure you want. It's always appropriate and recommended to send a thank you note to acknowledge the reporter who covered your story.

Internet Marketing

When you are creating your communication messages, you'll find that internet marketing is the least expensive and most interesting way of connecting with your target market. Internet marketing has changed and grown in the last 10-15 years. The changes come so fast that it's difficult to keep up with them. I would suspect that in the next few years, what you are doing now may be obsolete. That's how quickly things change in cyberspace.

The important thing to know about internet marketing is that it is just one aspect of your marketing campaign. Some people find that internet marketing works best for them. Other business owners find that a combination of traditional and internet marketing are the best solutions. Smart marketers cover all their bases and attract new clients from various media.

Note: I name web sites throughout this section that were introduced to me through professional business organizations.

I do not endorse any vendor. Always investigate anyone with whom you do business.

Consider these options when it comes to successful internet marketing:

1. Email marketing
2. Web site and search engine optimization
3. Social Media
   A. Blog
   B. Facebook
   C. Twitter
   D. You Tube
   E. LinkedIn
   F. Flickr

Email Marketing

Email marketing is a great way to stay in touch with those clients who only visit your salon once a month or every three months. Email correspondence is an accepted way of communication and many people look forward to receiving a weekly or monthly email, especially if there's something in it for them. Your business information and promotions go right into the customer's email box, which can be more effective than other forms of marketing... such as blogs. Although you may consider directing email readers to your blog where they can interact with you between appointments.

Start building your email list by asking all clients for their contact information. You probably already have their phone number and address, so why not their email address? Make a list of all your contacts and divide clients into a group list. This is another way of communicating with clients and staying present in their minds.

Your weekly or monthly email should offer good information: something educational or something free. Many companies offer coupons or the chance to enter a contest. You could offer a favorite recipe, shopping tips, beauty tips, community news or anything that might inform, delight or entertain.

Your email program may only allow you to send out a certain number of group emails. Go beyond that and your email company thinks you are a spammer. The downside is that they may not send your emails at all.

There are *email marketing service providers* who offer software to help you email large amounts of enewsletters, share them on social networking sites, integrate with services you already use, and track your results. MailChimp.com was suggested. It's free, and there are charges as your list increases. You may also consider Constant Contact, iContact, VerticalResponse, and cooleremail. Review their web sites to learn if they are a match for your needs and budget.

Create a Web Site

Before you build your web site there are initial steps to take.

1. Get a Domain Name: Most business people find value in having their own domain name and a web site to promote their businesses. Purchasing a domain name or URL is the first place to start. The domain name is the name of your business (or something similar) that must be chosen and purchased from a web hosting company. The initials URL means Uniform Resource Locator, and it is an identifier of your web site address, which is http://www.hairunlimited.com and points people to your web site when they either click on your link or type your name into a search engine such as Google, Yahoo, Bing or any other.

For instance, your salon name might be Hair Unlimited, which was the name of my salon for fourteen years. Go to an internet hosting company such as GoDaddy.com or Dreamhost. com, AwardSpace.com or others and see if that name is available. If it is available, sign up and purchase that name. It belongs to you to use as long as you pay a yearly fee, which is around $10.00. The fee is renewable each year. Let's suppose that the name was already taken, and it is. Then you would need to look for other appropriate words to use or you would modify the word in some way, such as hair_unlimited.com, or hairunlimited.biz or some other combination of words.

It's best to get your own business name, but if it isn't available, you might use initials, your slogan or a term/words that appeal to you, and define your business.

2. Design Your Web Site with the Client in Mind: Once you have your internet address, you will be able to build a web site that gives all pertinent information and is easy to navigate. Earlier I mentioned that a web site is essentially your brochure in cyber-space. It's beyond the scope of this book to tell you how to build a web site, but I can help you with the components. The *Home Page* is the landing page where potential clients will get a first impression of your business. Typically you give all your up front information on this page and provide links to additional information located on other pages. Your home page usually has your company name, and logo at the top where it is easily seen and identified. You might have some pertinent photos of your salon, staff or illustrations and some copy describing what your business is about and what problems you solve. There might be some testimonials from happy, satisfied customers and a list of products you sell. Look around at the web sites of other salons to determine what appeals to you and what should not be included. You may want to seek the services of a professional web site developer.

3. Know What You Want the Site to Do: The most important thing about a web site is to determine in advance what you want the site to do? Are you selling products or services? Are you offering information about specialized products and unique services, a map to your location or coupons? Will it sell your image? Will you shoot a video with you talking about your products and services? Do you plan on selling products online? If so, you will need a "shopping cart system." The more complicated your web site is, the more it will cost to get it up and running.

I suggest asking friends and associates to recommend a good web site developer and get several estimates. Think it through before you do anything, and remember it is a work in progress. Anything can be changed and should be changed periodically. Remember to include ways for viewers to contact you either through your email address, phone number and/or social media.

4. Go For Extra Added Benefits: Some of the things that make your web site more valuable are incentives, clear product photos, links that work and interesting and relevant information. A nice balance of text and photos is appealing.

5. Get Help if You Need It: There are businesses that offer either a free or low cost web site that you build yourself. Two suggestions are coffeecup.com and dreamtemplate.com. Godaddy also has some very simple web page templates. They are free if you purchase a domain name and/or web hosting from them.

Search Engines

Once your web site is active it's time to list it with search engines such as Google, Yahoo, bing.com (Microsoft Network), Ask.com, Teoma.com, altavista, excite, HotBot, Lycos, AOL search, and others. The goal is to be listed on the first page where readers can find you, click on your link, visit your site and hopefully purchase a product or service from you. I recommend a web site called: http://www.thesearchenginelist.com/ for all the places you can list your web site and more. You can learn how web search engines work through the free online encyclopedia – http://www.wikipedia.org

Search Engine Optimization (SEO)

Search engine optimization does exactly what it promises to do … it optimizes your web site to generate leads and make sales. The goal is for your web site to rank highly in the search engines so visitors find your web site. Here is how it works. There are two primary types of SEO: organic key words and pay-per-click.

Search engines and visitors find you according to the organic keywords they key in to the search box, and the same keywords you use on your web site or through paid advertisements. With that, the connection is made.

Google and other search engines have an index very much like an index in the back of a cookbook. You read the index to find a specific recipe or piece of knowledge. Google indexes all key words so when someone enters that word into their search box, your web site (with that key word) appears in the listing, preferably on the first page … the page that gets the most views. Most people lose interest after 4-5 pages.

1. Think in Terms of "Keywords:"

Those keywords always describe something that the viewer is searching for … about the salon business or the location in which your salon is located. They are basically trying to narrow down their options. Let's say a consumer is looking for a hair color salon in Chicago that also uses Redken products. Some examples of keywords are: hair salon, hair cut (Chicago), beauty salon San

Francisco, Redken salon, children's salon, hair color, men's hair cuts, Paul Mitchell, shampoo. When they enter "hair color salon, Chicago, Redken," websites with those keywords will show up on the page in bold. Using parentheses also focuses the search.

When writing the copy for your website, be certain to choose unique key words that perfectly describe your business, products or services and use those words consistently in the text/copy on your web site pages and in your titles. Don't overdo it, but definitely include them as much as possible.

Secret: It's important to use your keywords in the html code behind your web site in meta tags or title tags. Doing so may give you a higher search ranking. You or your web site builder can write them in.

2. Viewers are Searching for Something:

Once viewers look down the list of choices, they click on the links that interest them ... hopefully yours. Get the advantage by using your keywords in an appealing phrase or testimonial on your web site. If it's chosen by the *search engine spider* the phrase will appear with your link. As viewers read down the page, they'll scan for information they want and when they find it, "bingo" ... they click on your link.

For example, I went to Google's search box and I typed in "hair salon San Francisco." The two bolded keywords in the listing were "hair salon" and "San Francisco." The first thing that came up were seven local hair salons (who pay to have their contact information and links show up first), then a variety of unpaid advertisements and local salons.

A salon named "Cinta" came up on the first page, and both keywords were bolded in the listing. It said, "Cinta Salon and day spa in **San Francisco** holds a team of professional stylists ready to serve you with premium **hair** makeup waxing and new age techniques." Any potential client searching the page for a hair salon would be attracted to that phrase, especially the word *premium*.

3. Using Pay-Per-Click Advertisements:

On the top and the right side of the search page are "pay per click" links and advertisements. Those salons pay a price every time someone clicks on their link. They set up a budget with the search engine, not to exceed a predetermined amount of money. Every time someone clicks on their link money is deducted from their account. It might be only ten or twenty five cents or it might be more.

Read those listings to find what words appeal to you and would persuade you to click on their link and view their web site. I clicked on the "Rudy Sandoval Hair Artist" link and found an effective web site. Take the time to explore the ways other salon owners represent themselves. You will be impressed. Remember, they are your competition so you'll want to make a good impression too.

Another effective tool is SEO tools. Google Analytics allows you to measure your advertising (ROI) return on investment as well as track your flash, video, and social networking applications. It gives you rich insights into your website traffic and marketing effectiveness. Check with Google for details about their programs. See what visitors are doing on your web site. http://www.google.com/analytics/

4. To Get a Higher Ranking:

You need professionally researched keyword phrases, lots of content, back links (these are links from other web sites to yours), proper coding and descriptions on your web site, links to social media, videos and podcast, and a web site that has been consistent and available for a long time.

Social Media

Social media is a communicative media for social interaction using web based and mobile technology. Social media started out as a media where individuals could meet, communicate and interact in cyberspace. Individuals could interact with people anywhere in the world without limitation as to their location. As long as one has a mobile device, and/or computer and an internet connection, they could talk and share information. What I like most about social media is that it gives everyone a voice, a critical aspect of a democratic society. It's long overdue, necessary and impactful. Building relationships and loyalty are the main goals of social media to the business community.

Businesses of all sizes have gotten on the bandwagon and often use consumer generated media to talk about their businesses and get their messages out to the masses. The most popular social media sites are now Facebook, Twitter, You Tube, LinkedIn, Technorati, flickr, MySpace, Digg, StumbleUpon and a host of others. Take some time to study these social media sites to determine if joining the conversation holds the key to your success.

There is definitely a protocol when using social media and some important do's and don'ts:

1. Do: Before you register on every site, keep your marketing goals in mind. Learn what the site offers and if it's a fit for your business. Who are their customers, and will they fit with what you have to offer? You may or may not reach the potential clients you desire. If not, you are wasting your time and energy.

2. Don't: One of the most important don'ts in social media is pitching your business without offering quality content. Remember that social media is about building relationships, and providing interesting and informative content. It's about people teaching other people what they know, outside of a standard learning organization like a high school or college.

3. Do: It's a great forum for discussion on many topics and when yours comes up, you are expected to contribute and be open minded.

4. Don't: Another don't is to reveal too much about your personal life. It's best to keep a professional stance at all times.

Secret: Remember one thing about social media. This is about "people talking to and about people/businesses." It's interactive communication, and you have the opportunity to not only express yourself but direct the conversation about YOU to be a positive one.

Tip: Don't fret if you get negative feedback on your blog, web site, Facebook page or email. While it may be painful, it gives you an opportunity to improve, and that's worth its weight in gold.

Create a Blog

Many business people will have a *Blog* along with their web site or in place of their web site. A blog is a web log or a written log of entries pertaining to one's business. It allows you to have a voice in your community.

The entries are either important information, opinions, facts or interesting commentary that you want your readers to know. It's all about self-expression and sharing expertise. Blogs are always informational and often interactive, allowing visitors to leave comments.

A typical blog sometimes combines business information, images, and links to other blogs or web sites. Some people use them as a personal online diary, but you might have a different purpose for your salon. You could talk about these updates in your business:

- New products and services
- New staff members
- Special events at your salon
- Special promotions
- Changes in your hours or location
- Your local community
- Anything interesting that happens from day to day or week to week in your salon

If you live in a small, close knit community where a lot of people know each other, it might be appropriate to mention information pertaining to your clients: who is graduating, getting married, having a baby, moving to a new home or going off to college. Many people like to see their names and photos in print or online. This media gives everyone a chance at celebrity. Make sure your write ups are entertaining and engaging ... and readers will return. Your blog could be a forum where many people participate, but only if it's appropriate and you handle it in good taste. You can create a free blog at Google. com/blogspot, WordPress.com, blog.com, or blogger.com. Some of these blogs have templates and are easy to implement.

The web site Technorati.com is a technology web site directly related to the blogging community or what they call the "blogosphere." They list the top 100 blogs and give you statistics and information related to blogging. It's a good resource for finding trends and staying in touch with the blogging community. They answer the "who, what and how" of this popular technology.

Join Facebook

Facebook is one of the most popular social media websites in the United States and abroad. Just about everyone seems to have their own pages. The site was originally designed for college students, but eventually became popular for children, teenagers, parents, singles, grandparents and business owners.

Go to the Facebook web site and sign up for a free profile. Get a Facebook account and a fan page. Fan pages are specifically for businesses, and this media gives you an opportunity to post information about your business that goes directly to your fan's computers. The great thing about it is that it's a free and easy way to keep clients abreast of what you are doing, offering or selling. You can post photos of events at your salon and share information without any cost.

Tip: Remember, social media is about building relationships, and not about shameless self-promoting.

Join Twitter

Twitter is a social media site that allows users to tweet or text each other, but the technology only allows you to type in 140 characters. This means your messages must be short, sweet and succinct. The good news is that it's also fast to send a message, and its quick to read. There's no getting chatty with this media. Some people like Twitter for sending brief messages to friends, family and interested customers.

The whole key to success with Twitter and most social media is to not be boring. Send vibrant messages with a link to your web site. Make it unique and people will follow you on Twitter. Let your clients know about product and service specials, new styles or cuts, or your open house. How about your new digital coffee center that makes latte's, cappuccino's and macchiato's?

You Tube

You Tube is one of the most popular social media web sites and cost effective vehicles for broadcasting your business. If you are good in front of a camera, this option could be for you. Create an original and engaging video of yourself or your business for the general public. Make it interesting and entertaining, and it may go viral. Going viral is a term used for a unique video that is passed on from person to person until it gets noticed by the masses. The potential for national popularity is astounding. You might remember the British singer Susan Boyle, whose video went viral and she became an international hit. Go to You Tube and watch the top videos for clues to what goes viral.

Creating a video can give potential customers an inside look at your new, great salon or an inside line on stylists who have something exciting to share. You must be credible, enthusiastic and likeable. Share what you know in a way that inspires potential clients to want more. There are an endless variety of gimmicks you can use on a You Tube video. You can educate and train people, and make a pitch for your service or product.

The marketing messages most suited to video are demonstrations, testimonials, entertainment, training and your shining personality. Use any combination of these ideas. According to my research, demonstrations are the most effective ways to get new clients through video technology.

Create some "before and after" videos to show what you and your staff are capable of accomplishing. Remember to get an in-person video testimonial from those individuals or others.

The more happy and excited they are, the better. As a side note, you might want to offer the videotaped client a free service, a gift or monetary payment for their time and permission. It's not a bribe, but a gift for participation. Make sure its authentic or it may backfire on you, hurting your reputation. Video marketing is based on trust and you don't want to destroy that bond.

You can spend as little as $100 on a Flip camera or purchase a more expensive video camera to create professional videos for You Tube or your own web site. You can spend as little as 4 minutes or longer to get your message across. Depending on the complexity of your message, you can do it yourself or hire the services of a professional for a more quality presentation. Always find a home for your video on your web site and send links to everyone with whom you are connected.

Another advantage of using You Tube is that there are tutorials on just about everything. That makes it one of a business person's most valuable resources.

There are companies who offer professional video editing to make you look good. You can use a local vendor or a business called pixability.com, which was recommended by a small business technology company. See their web site for prices and packages.

Join LinkedIn

The word on the street is, "It's all in who you know." There is no better place to make business connections than LinkedIn. This is a great opportunity for business owners to set up a profile and connect with other business owners or potential customers. People use LinkedIn to get jobs, find resources and connect with anyone who may assist you in getting your foot in the door at another company.

Go to the LinkedIn website, sign up and create a profile. The company will send you updates about people in your network who meet other people, making it a valuable resource.

Join Flickr

Flickr is an online management and sharing application that allows you to tell your story with photos, and people can make comments. This could be a good web site to place your best hair-style/haircut photos, as well as photos to show off your newly remodeled salon or anything newsworthy.

Note: This is not the final word on internet marketing or social media. As I said earlier in "internet marketing," the media changes at a rapid pace. While this media is basically free, it is more successful with a good dose of time and effort.

Step 9. Launch Your Campaign

Once you have all your communication messages ready to go, you are ready to launch your marketing campaign and take your business to the next level. Follow the Market Planning Guide for outlining your campaign for the year.

Market Planning Guide

This Market Planning Guide is an example that will allow you to view your promotions for the entire year.

Promotion	Media	Objective	Timeline	Budget
Jan: New Year's Sale	Flyers, local newspaper	Sell shopworn products	2 week sale	$125
Feb. Valentine's Day	Coupons, radio	Promote hair color, sell fragrances and jewelry	3 day sale	$175-200

Promotion	Media	Objective	Timeline	Budget
March: Salon Anniversary	Newspaper	Public relations activity - Increase retail sales by 10%, increase traffic by 30%	1 week 3/15 - 3/22	$250
April				
May				

Step 10. Marketing Evaluation

It is important to rate the effectiveness of your marketing campaign. Ask yourself if you are satisfied with your marketing and promotional efforts? Were the results what you expected? Did you get new clients and increased sales? Is your community more aware of your presence and your expertise? How could you make it better?

After each promotion, evaluate whether or not it was worthwhile. Keep an advertising ledger from year to year and note which promotions you did, why it did or didn't work, how you could do it differently or better, and who participated to make it successful? Remember that not everyone responds immediately. A potential client may see your advertisement, and may not need that service at the moment. They may choose to make an appointment the next time.

Continue to strengthen a productive campaign. You will eventually need to find a fresh approach to promoting your services and products as people, products, and markets change. But don't give up on your current campaign until you are sure the market has been depleted.

How to Change Direction When Necessary

I don't know anyone who has a crystal ball, allowing you to see into the future. There are steps you can take to safeguard your position. You can develop an alternative direction to go in the event that your salon needs to expand or perhaps downsize.

Effective owners or managers must be willing to choose alternatives when opportunity knocks. For example, you may now envision your salon specifically as a hair cutting salon. However, market conditions or competition may change. You may need to completely change your direction in order to survive. That's the time when it's best to take a survey and ask clients what more you could do to serve them? Remember, it's all about them. If you have the space and capital you may want to incorporate those requested services or products. Ask yourself: is it realistic, is it sensible, is it profitable, and is it necessary?

For Cosmetology Students

Cosmetology students - pay attention to your education first:

- Learn as many skills as you can in trade school. Get your technical training, ensuring you will pass your exams and get your state license.
- Serve an apprenticeship at the kind of salon you'd like to own. Work for people who can teach you priceless skills.
- Take an advanced cutting and styling class.
- Take advanced hair color classes.
- A management, small business or supervisory course at your local community college would be a smart business decision and a good way in which to plan for your future.
- Attending a business development seminar would give you some valuable insights.

- Attend Cosmetology Seminars, Trade Shows and Conferences. Business and motivational classes are offered specifically for this field.
- Your local library has start-up manuals for various businesses. They aren't always updated, but can still give you some insights.
- Find a mentor. Ask a local salon owner if you can visit the salon to see how the operations work. Building relationships is key and you can learn a lot from hanging out and watching what to do and not do.

Tip: You can have all the good intentions in the world, but if you don't follow through and make the effort and act, then your dreams are just that, dreams and wishes. They can come true, but it does require action. Every day, think one small thought, take one small step towards your goals. Once you get some momentum going, you'll begin to experience the fun and joy of accomplishment and satisfaction.

In Conclusion

Effective marketing is crucial to the success of your salon. All of the information in this book is designed to help you get a handle on how to make your salon more successful. This chapter guides you through all the specifics and brings them together to your advantage.

Notes:

CHAPTER NINETEEN
Quitting Your Business

Henry Ford, America's premier entrepreneur, said,
"Failure is the opportunity to begin again, more intelligently."

Cut the Cord

When business doesn't go well, sometimes the best and only course of action is to cut the cord or shut down entirely and begin anew. Start again with a different purpose, mission statement, and goals. Hire a whole new set of employees which fit into your new business plan, and in turn attract an entirely different market. You must have the finances, determination and passion needed to begin again. You probably learned valuable information from your earlier mistakes. That in itself could lead you to newfound success.

Sometimes entrepreneurs merely get tired of their business. The salon may continue to be successful, but the entrepreneur has run out of energy. The salon owner may feel there is no room to grow, or their business has reached its peak. Burned out owners have had enough of that type of business and desire to try something else. They may sell the business, close the doors one day, or pass it along to a family member.

When it's time to move on, let go and move on. It is in your own best interests as well as for the employees and clients.

After all is said and done, you may find that you make more

money working for someone else, if it is only money that is important to you. Let other salon owners have all the headaches and responsibilities. You can put your tools away for the evening and go home.

How to Sell Your Salon

Your best option, when deciding to go out of business, is to sell the salon as a whole unit. There are a few options for selling your business: use a realtor, sell it yourself, or sell it to an employee, friend or family member. It's a difficult decision to sell your salon. It's been your baby/business and like most entrepreneurs you've put your blood, sweat and tears into it. It's nice if you can make a profit and live off of that for a while until you find your new direction. I tried several times to sell my last salon without much luck. People knew I was successful, but either didn't believe my income was as high as it was or just wanted it for free. My lease was up, and I was ready to move on, so I sold my salon on contract to one of my best employees, whom I had trained throughout the years. I had unwittingly groomed her to take over. I passed my baby along to her and knew it was in good hands. Our clients were also well taken care of, so I was able to walk away feeling good about the whole situation.

If you must sell the equipment piece by piece (equipment depreciates rapidly), you won't get what it is worth. My first salon did not sell as a complete business, so I was forced to sell each item separately. I found this to be an uncomfortable and time-consuming process. The hydraulic chairs are the quickest to go and easiest to sell. The rest you may sell at a loss unless you attract someone, like I did, who was getting ready to open her first salon. Potential salon owners on a budget are always looking for good used equipment.

If you decide to take your equipment to auction, the best price comes from people battling over desired pieces. I saw incredibly nice equipment go for next to nothing at an auction. The former owner was beside himself with disappointment.

In Conclusion

Quitting or selling your business and going in another direction is a situation you may experience at some point. There comes a time when you may have to let go and move from one chapter of your life to another. The new chapter may be retirement, a new career, or whatever new adventure life has in store for you. Allow your salon experience to make you a wiser person, and take that wisdom with you to your next adventure.

A Note from the Author

I pray you are grateful for your cosmetology career and salon business experience. It's a wonderful creative and social outlet and, if you allow it to happen, it can enrich your life in more ways than you can count.

The salon life was good for me for that half of my life, and I am eternally grateful to my mother Tillie for pointing me in that direction. It gave me unlimited opportunities for growth. Her reward was a lifetime of free haircuts, styles and color. I expect that was her plan. She was happy and so was I.

I trust that you will receive a great deal of wisdom and direction from these pages, and that you will implement them in a way that makes your salon business easier to manage. May you make it BIG in the salon business!

Good Luck and Best Wishes,
Linda L. Chappo

About the Author

Linda L. Chappo, a veteran of the cosmetology profession, graduated from Heim Beauty School in Gary, Indiana and received her Indiana license in 1967. She worked at the Best Beauty Shop and then Gerald's Coiffures for the next six years. Linda was present throughout the 1960's and 70's hair revolution ... teased updo's, the bubble, the rise of Vidal Sassoon, Twiggy cut, the shag, the wedge, and the shift from razor cuts to shears.

Linda stepped up her game in 1975 by opening her first salon, "Hair Unlimited," and then another in 1980. Fourteen years later, after achieving undreamed of success, she was ready to explore other grounds.

Linda's desire to write became manifest in a book about the hair salon business. Linda offers a personal account of the challenges and lessons of salon life.

Linda moved to California in 1991 and found her way back to the salon industry while getting a degree in graphic communications and certifications in alternative healing arts. After getting her California cosmetology license she worked at Mr. Eckhard Salon at the Fairmont Hotel and Just Cuts in San Francisco.

Linda later founded the West Coast Business Academy and taught small business marketing classes. She also wrote a marketing book for small business owners (which began in her salon book) endorsed by marketing guru Jay Conrad Levinson entitled *"Full Strength Marketing: How You can use Your Hidden Strengths, Break Through Inner Barriers, and Raise Your Profits"* published by QuickBreakThrough Publishing. This book has contributing articles by 24 top marketers including Brian Tracy, Jill Lublin, Marc Allen, and Paul Gillin. Both books are available as a printed book or ebook on Amazon.com.

Linda's mission is now to share what she's learned throughout the years as both a salon owner/entrepreneur and sales/marketing expert. She offers classes/seminars in salon start up and salon marketing. You can reach Linda at lchappo@aol.com or 510-524-6014 for more information.

Made in the USA
San Bernardino, CA
09 October 2013